THE FRONT PORCH

Stories from the Soul of San Antonio

VINCENT T. DAVIS

FOREWORD BY CARY CLACK

MAVERICK BOOKS / TRINITY UNIVERSITY PRESS

San Antonio, Texas

Published by Maverick Books, an imprint of Trinity University Press
San Antonio, Texas 78212

The columns in this book originally appeared in the *San Antonio Express-News*, reprinted courtesy of the Hearst Corporation.

Book design by BookMatters, Berkeley
Cover design by Robert Salinas, DVS Design
Author photo by Josie Norris

978-1-59534-334-5 paperback
978-1-59534-335-2 ebook

Trinity University Press strives to produce its books using methods and materials in an environmentally sensitive manner. We favor working with manufacturers that practice sustainable management of all natural resources, produce paper using recycled stock, and manage forests with the best possible practices for people, biodiversity, and sustainability. The press is a member of the Green Press Initiative, a nonprofit program dedicated to supporting publishers in their efforts to reduce their impacts on endangered forests, climate change, and forest-dependent communities.

The paper used in this publication meets the minimum requirements of the American National Standard for Information Sciences—Permanence of Paper for Printed Library Materials, ansi 39.48–1992.

CIP data on file at the Library of Congress

30 29 28 27 26 | 5 4 3 2 1

To Diane, who always believed

For the four family members

whose foundation I stand on—

my mother, Valeria Cardona-Trinidad;

my grandmother, Lela Mae Preer Hicks;

and my great-grandparents,

Willie Lou and Theodore H. Martin

Contents

THOSE WITHOUT A VOICE

OF COMBAT, CAMARADERIE, AND COUNTRY

Foreword

CARY CLACK

When I think of Vince Davis I'm reminded of front porches. In my mind and experience, front porches are synonymous with storytelling, and Davis is a master storyteller. Whether through spoken or written words, he can tell a good story, so it's easy to imagine him on a front porch regaling those around him. But an underrated talent for being a good storyteller is being a good listener, not only to the narrative being told but to the pauses, hesitations, and vocal inflections. Davis is an exceptional story listener. Part of my front porch imagery of him is him sitting, leaning forward with elbows on knees, and an empathetic nodding of his head, watching closely.

Stories are meant to be shared, and in that sense they are like batons in a relay race passed from one person to another, one generation to another, one culture to another. Through seeking out, listening, and a passionate dedication to his writing craft, Davis has taken, carried, and passed on that baton of listening and storytelling. Communities are rich repositories of stories waiting to be discovered and told, listened to and shared. Davis has been mining San Antonio's rich vein of stories throughout a stellar career of nearly thirty years at the *San Antonio Express-News*, a career few people, Davis included, imagined that he would have.

He was married with a daughter when he retired from the Air Force after serving twenty-two years and enrolled in San Antonio

College, which had one of the best community college journalism programs in the country. While studying and working for the campus newspaper, Davis began working nights and weekends for the *Express-News* as a part-time editorial assistant. He later earned a bachelor's degree in communication design from Texas State University in San Marcos. As his role and writing opportunities at the *Express-News* increased, it was evident that this laid-back, affable veteran had not only an extraordinary work ethic and drive to excel but an easy way of connecting with people, learning their stories, and a deft, descriptive writing style in relaying them.

A community is a sum of its people and is understood and comes to understand itself through the stories of all of its people. *The Front Porch* collects some of Davis's finest work, a mosaic of the community composed of individual profiles of San Antonians. To open this book is akin to sitting on San Antonio's front porch and listening to its many stories. By the time you close the cover, you will have a better understanding of the city and its character and diversity. You will come to care about people you never knew existed, people you may have passed or caught a glimpse of on the street and wondered what their story was. People like Michael Anthony "Mike" Ruiz, who supports his family by cleaning windows and spends hours each day walking the streets looking for work. Or Gloria Bryant, the "tea cake lady of San Antonio," whose cookies "are like warm sunshine that melts in your mouth"; Lucia Lozano, a ninety-one-year-old designer and dressmaker; and the Ghost Town Survivors, teenage gang members who as senior citizens bring Christmas joy to West Side families. You'll enjoy the simple pleasure of Rodney Castillo fishing and bonding with his ten-year-old daughter Bryanna; and Dominic and Moses, two large cats protecting Mission Espada.

These pages resonate with the sounds of music, singing, and dancing; the tastes of taquerias and soul food restaurants; and the tales of families, African American enclaves, and Spanish American League baseball. The pieces included here reacquaint readers with such San

Antonio institutions as Elf Louise and Ruben's Tamales. But Davis also pulls back the veil to tell us his own family's stories, rich narratives that reveal how he became the person, husband, father, and writer that he is. There's a beautiful Mother's Day tribute to his late mother, Valeria Cardona-Trinidad, and a wonderfully sketched lesson on mortality from his great-grandmother, Willie Lou Martin, known as Madea.

Then there's his great-grandfather, the most direct source of Davis's talent. In "Granddaddy Passed on the Magical Art of Spinning Tales," he writes:

> Theodore H. Martin had a thick mustache and hair combed back with Old 97 hair grease. Smoking Hav-A-Tampa cigars, he spun stories that transported listeners to war-torn lands, dark country roads, and fire-lit cabins. Listeners left doubled over from laughter and dabbing tears away. I can still see my great-grandfather sitting in his den in Columbus, Georgia, regaling fellow World War II army veterans and relatives with outrageous tales that defied belief. Adult family members called him Sarge. Fellow Army veterans called him Mr. Martin. My great-grandmother called him Pietro. To my sisters and me, he was simply Granddaddy. But he had another name: storyteller. It was from Granddaddy that I learned the magical sway of stories.

Davis learned well. Let's gather on this storyteller's front porch and enjoy his craft.

Introduction

The stories collected here are the result of one thing—the kindness of strangers.

For the past twenty-five years I've had the privilege of sharing tales of folks from in and around San Antonio. Daily assignments at the *San Antonio Express-News* took me to settings I'd never have been welcomed to, I believe, without a badge hanging from a lanyard that read "reporter."

That badge gave me access to people who celebrated life, who were on paths of recovery, carving out a living the best way they could.

I talked with folks from all walks of life from dawn till hours beyond midnight. An early morning pilgrimage from Helotes to a West Side church, midday on breast cancer prevention marathons around the Alamodome, and the dark of night amid raucous Spurs championship celebrations.

Folks invited the newspaper's photographers and me into their homes to listen to memories of loved ones who'd passed, good deeds done decades ago, and lives lived for more than a century.

You'll find stories here of people who took advantage of second chances, like the Ghost Town Survivors, a group of former West Side gang members who gave back to those in need in their old neighborhood. You'll read the story of Sam Greco, whose life began and ended with Saint Francis, patron saint of Italian Americans.

And you'll learn about descendants of Black freedmen, deep in the Seguin countryside, who celebrated more than 150 years of worship at a church founded by their ancestors.

There is also a sampling here of many stories from military veterans across San Antonio, dubbed Military City USA. You'll read of how, during World War II, a white bomber crew happened upon the then-unknown Tuskegee Airmen after making an emergency landing in Italy. In another piece, the soldiers of Bravo Company, 2nd Platoon invite us into their gathering in honor of a comrade slain in the Vietnam War. And you'll listen in with me as an English World War II bride weaves a tale of falling in love with her husband, Manuel Barrera, amid a clash of cultures and discrimination.

Among the articles are several "San Antonio Story" columns, which were featured every Monday in the metro section of the *Express-News*.

I hadn't yet started school when I first heard riveting stories from my great-grandfather Theodore H. Martin, a tale spinner who personified the power of storytelling. It never occurred to me that I'd follow in his footsteps, albeit in a different way. A World War II veteran, he spun stories that inspired my family and doubled us over in laughter with each telling. With a cigar wedged in his mouth, he transported us from the family den in Columbus, Georgia, to distant lands and dark country roads deep in the South. There were tales that included a man thought dead, come back to life in a horse-drawn wagon on the way to the mortician's parlor.

Each story put us at the scene with descriptions and color that brought the story to life. It's a technique I've also tried to use. I've been fortunate to apply this technique and many others to writing since I became a journalist in 1998. When I retired from the U.S. Air Force after a twenty-two-year career, I set out to get an associate's degree in graphic design from San Antonio College. An index card on a corkboard altered that plan.

It was a request for an editorial cartoonist at the *Ranger*, a student-run newspaper. When I went to the interview, Chester "Chet" Hunt, chair of the college journalism and photography department, scanned my portfolio. He said the work was fine but wondered if I would be interested in learning about encapsulating an issue with an illustration. I agreed to take on the job, and he put me to work that night.

Tricia Buchhorn taught me how to use a Mac computer and develop an eye for stories. Hunt, Irene Abrego, and Marianne Odom taught me the basics of reporting and, like my great-grandfather, how to tell a story that mirrored a moment in time.

It's an honor to have a collection of stories published by Trinity University Press, which includes books on its list by colleagues Joe Holley and Cary Clack. Both have had an impact on my writing career. Joe may not remember this, but when I was first starting out, he stopped and asked me a question that set the wheels rolling for me writing stories in my voice rather than following a more traditional by-the-numbers format. He asked what type of stories I wanted to write, and I said whatever story I was covering. Then he asked *how* I wanted to tell a story, and that question shook my senses. I still thank Joe for taking time to encourage a novice to stretch and use all his senses to tell a story, just like my great-grandfather did in his den in Columbus.

Cary taught me to write with heart, to reveal the humanity that beats within each of us, no matter what our station or status. He's always been available to offer sound counsel and a listening ear when I was dealing with the complex mysteries of professional and personal situations.

Armed with all this training and support, I hit the streets of San Antonio. Interviews often took place on the run as I tried to get quotes and descriptions while writing on deadline. Former deputy metro editor Monica Markel gave me and the paper's photojournalists license to comb the city for tales tucked away from the daily blur of hustle and bustle. Giving a voice to people who rarely saw their name in print, people from every city zip code, became part of our mission. We heard from readers who said these stories gave them a respite from reports of crime, corruption, and political chaos. One reader emailed to say, "These kinds of stories are so important as it is what tethers us together as a community."

This collection is my way of saying thank you to the many folks who took time to talk to a stranger, a reporter with a badge, who was and is humbled to have had the honor to listen to and share their stories.

FAITH FOREVER

Hattitude

Sitting in the back of Bethel A.M.E. Church on a hot Sunday morning, Sister Calvin Marie Dukes is a portrait of style. She wears a turquoise straw hat complete with rippling brim and a swath of white silk ribbon wrapped around the crown, fastened in the back with a blue butterfly cloth pin. The colors of her dress match her hat to a T. Rocking a restless young boy on her lap, she holds her head high as shouts of "Amen!" fill the room. Sitting in pews ahead of her, at least twenty women wearing hats of various sizes, styles, and colors nod as the choir sings "heaven is looking down on me."

Shafts of light shine through stained-glass windows, casting a golden glow on the hats like crowns on queens. Similar scenes play out every Sunday in churches across the country. For many African American women, wearing a hat in church is an honored tradition. It reflects a certain attitude. Or, as it's been called, "hattitude."

For decades the practice of wearing hats has been recognized as a cultural phenomenon. Books have chronicled the tradition. In the early 2000s photographer Michael Cunningham and author Craig Marberry were featured on CBS's *Sunday Morning* and on National Public Radio's *Weekend Edition* with Liane Hansen. In their book, *Crowns: Portraits of Black Women in Church Hats*, Marberry and Cunningham note that African societies believe the head is the storehouse of wisdom and the entry and exit point for the spirit.

This belief led to special decoration, including wraps, braids, and hairstyles, being worn in African culture. Pride of presentation during worship services became a tradition of African American women wearing expressive hats. Many women were raised to wear a hat and gloves to Sunday school, and if the Sunday outfit didn't include a hat it was considered incomplete. The only time a woman's head was bare was when she sang in the choir. In the 1800s, bonnets were women's head cover of choice. Most African American women wore wide-brimmed straw hats to block out sunlight while laboring in the fields, and some wrapped a cloth under their hats to soak up sweat. When it was time for worship, they gathered, wearing the best of what they had.

At the turn of the century bonnets gave way to big-brimmed hats decorated with feathers, beads, ribbons, and veils. After World War II factory-made hats were plentiful—at affordable prices. In the early 1960s First Lady Jacqueline Kennedy reignited interest in hats, as did Diana, the Princess of Wales, in the 1980s and 1990s. And through all those years, African American women never strayed from the tradition of wearing hats to church.

Ruth Jones, fashion coordinator at Julian Gold, a women's clothing store in Olmos Park, is a hat aficionado. She says that, for many years, African American women shopped at Frost Bros., her former workplace, for church hats. When Frost closed in 1989, Jones's loyal customers followed her to Julian Gold for her fashion expertise and the store's expressive hats. "The bigger the hat, the more expensive they are," Jones says.

In 2001 hat prices at Julian Gold ranged from less than $100 to $500. Casey Bush, executive director of the Headwear Information Bureau in New York City, says an informal survey shows price increases on casual and dress hats. "There's been less demand for hats that retail under $100," Bush says. "Moderate-priced dress hats have suffered the last year or two."

Jones makes another point: “A black woman is daring. She wants a hat that no one else has. It has to have pizazz.”

This leads some women to bypass factory-made hats for the services of a milliner. Bethel worshipper Barbara Siggers orders hats from a designer in New York. When she was a young girl, her mother stood her in front of a mirror, placed a hat on her head, and said, “Look, aren’t you beautiful!” She prefers a hat with a wide brim, which she says brings out her face.

The number of specialists in the Alamo City dwindled when hats became less fashionable in the 1970s. Now that custom-designed hats are in vogue, milliners are making a comeback, and though milliners Jennifer W. Bartelt and Ann Sance aren’t in the yellow pages, word of mouth keeps them busy. Neither woman uses traditional blocking equipment to create her hats. Both order plain hats and decorate them to customers’ specifications. And both women are avid hat lovers.

Bartelt started her service, Custom Millinery Design, a year ago, inspired by the belief that she could do as well as or better than department stores. She was tired of one-size-fits-all hats. Needle and thread are her tools of choice for attaching decorations. “It stays on permanently,” she says of the hat attachments. “It doesn’t disintegrate when it starts to rain.”

Customers from as far away as North Carolina have sought out Sance’s shop, Unique Hats by Ann, for special orders. Sance has a room in her house dedicated to the more than two hundred hats she’s collected over the years. “I used to keep them in boxes until I had too many,” she says.

When the owners of large collections die, the hats often end up in strangers’ homes unless special instructions are left in wills. “I see too many estate sales where hat collections are auctioned off,” Bartelt says. “I’m sure family and relatives would rather they [hats] stay with them.”

Lucille Brewer and Marcile Henson, ninety-year-old local twins, never go to church—at West End Baptist—without a hat. They've worn them since they were young girls, preferably ones "up off of the face." They recall their mother going every year to a millinery in Flatonia, where they lived, to buy two summer hats for the twins to wear to Sunday school. Today the fashion-conscious twins' collection includes hats made by Neiman Marcus, Frank Olive, and Christian Dior.

Sister Adell Polk is partial to hats by Jack McConnell because "they never go out of style." And she says you can't go wrong with a hat by Mr. John, a famous designer recognizable to most hat-wearers. "When you come into the house of the Lord, you always want to look your best," Polk says. "And give him your best."

Faith Bridges Gap

On Sunday mornings, praise team members line the stage in the Community Bible Church sanctuary, singing songs of thanks for one more day and deliverance from evil. Compact car–sized video screens on high walls bookend the stage, flashing images of the singers, orchestra, and choir as part of a twenty-first-century religious experience at the twenty-thousand-member church.

Performing before stadium-sized crowds is a familiar thing for one of the singers. In a past life, Ronnie Wilson helped write chart-topping songs with infectious rhythms that hooked fans and had them sliding onto dance floors. These days, there's a message in his music. These days, lyrics are more than mere words. Melodies are more than just tunes. And when his pastor recites the scripture, it's more like a revelation. These days, when Wilson sings, it's not fame he's seeking; it's the Holy Ghost. "I had to go out in the world and do the most damnable things and ruin many lives," said Wilson, age sixty-two. "Because God revealed things to me, I was able to say I'm sorry to a lot of those people."

With his two younger brothers, Wilson was a member of the Gap Band, a chart-topping funk group in the late 1970s and early 1980s. He was caught in the trappings of stardom and a $1,200-a-day cocaine habit. The Wilson brothers started the band in 1967 in Tulsa, Oklahoma, as the Greenwood, Archer, and Pine Streets Band, named after streets in their neighborhood. Ronnie played keyboards, middle brother Charlie sang lead, and younger brother Robert played bass—their talents honed after years playing instruments at their parents' insistence. The group, performing hits like "Burn Rubber," "Outstanding," and "You Dropped a Bomb on Me," appeared on popular music shows such as *Soul Train* and with top acts of the day such as Earth, Wind & Fire and Parliament-Funkadelic.

Wilson was known for his stylish glasses and thick mustache. He weighed 210 pounds and wore sequin-speckled, fringed outfits, calf-high boots, and cowboy hats. He credits a tongue-lashing by a drug dealer for leading him back to his Pentecostal beginnings. As he shed his old ways, he also shed his image for a look his fans would not recognize: bald and, because of health reasons, fifty pounds lighter.

Wilson became part of the music ministry at Community Bible Church when he joined in 2007 after attending one of the services. He came to San Antonio from Houston in 2006 when his wife was hired as a musical director at New Covenant Missionary Baptist Church. Minister of music and worship Ray Jones said Wilson, who also teaches a devotional class, has endeared himself to the congregation.

"They love to hear Ronnie sing; it's a real neat thing to watch," he said. "Here's a guy that made millions of dollars in the entertainment industry and nearly killed himself with drugs, and now he gets up every morning and works. Every morning at 9:30, they take a break, and there's Ronnie, opening up his Bible, speaking to the maintenance staff, and just being a minister."

Jones said the life of an entertainer can be a path to destructive behavior. "I think what happens is they get this sense of a high from doing their music. It's a rush that springs up in them this incredible energy. After performing they get in a pattern where they can't sleep well, they're jazzed up, and seek outside sources to bring them down and up."

Wilson's return to faith came twenty-seven years ago in Los Angeles after he called a dealer to buy drugs. "I'm kinda broke now," he told the dealer. The pusher cursed him and called him pitiful and everything but his name for two minutes. It was the last blow in a series of incidents that included being shot at and a suicide attempt.

He fell to his knees and pointed to the ceiling. "If you be God, I want you to take this drug habit away from me," he said. "Save me, and I'll serve you."

Wilson said that was the day he was reborn. He said if people want to see who he really is, they should read Ephesians 1:4. "Yesterday, I was a drug addict, alcoholic, womanizer, and adulterer. If you want to see who I really am, you have to go back one more day, past yesterday."

Wilson died on November 2, 2021, after a stroke. He was seventy-three. His brother Robert died of a heart attack on August 15, 2010. Brother Charlie, known as Uncle Charlie, is still touring and is a fixture on the R&B/hip-hop charts.

Pastor Ministers Those in Need on the East Side

About ten years ago, at the corner of Pine and Montana Streets in San Antonio, drug dealers entrenched at a dusty lot were surprised by the arrival of a minister without fear. They stared in disbelief as Pastor Shetigho Nakpodia strode over from her nearby church bearing food and the word of the Lord. Clad in a colorful head wrap and ankle-length dress from Africa, she scooped hot rice and beans onto paper plates for them and read scriptures about love and redemption. Prostitutes who lined the curbs were just as taken aback as she prayed for their salvation. She forgave those who had broken into the church building fourteen times and stolen musical instruments.

Despite setbacks, lack of resources, and naysayers, she has remained strong in her faith. Powered by a spiritual vision, Nakpodia began her ministry in 2010 when she used her savings to buy an old, empty chapel at 107 S. Pine Street that her brother Shokare, founder of DreamWeek, had brought to her attention. She named it Redeemer's Praise Church. She opened her doors to those without homes, the poor, and people suffering from anxiety and addictions. "That's what the Lord said to do," Nakpodia, age sixty-seven, said at the wooden altar where she started her East Side journey. "In my mind, there wasn't any other alternative."

To understand her mission, you have to go back to the late 1960s in Nigeria. Nakpodia, the oldest of twelve children, said her parents couldn't afford to care for her, so she was raised by her grandmother, who nurtured her faith. It sustained her as a child during the Biafra War when she had to walk streets scattered with the bodies of dead soldiers. It sustained her late at night as she hid beneath her bunk bed at Saint Maria Goretti secondary school as the ground shook from artillery shelling. And it sustained her after her twenty-five-year marriage ended in divorce and she lost her spacious home.

She went to work at an insurance company during the day and spent her nights studying to earn a master's degree in counseling from the University of Texas at San Antonio. Nakpodia raised her four children with the same philosophy of caring for others that her grandmother instilled in her.

Her teachings live on in her children: her oldest son, Mudia, thirty-four, a marketer in Seattle; and daughters Ovigwe, thirty-three, a fashion designer, and Sune, twenty-seven, an attorney in Waco. Her youngest son, Norie, recently resigned from his job to help at the church. He serves as floor manager of Redeemer's Praise. The thirty-one-year-old tall, soft-spoken man is on site every day, often late into the night, furthering his mother's cause.

Not long ago a hungry man living on the streets entered the sanctuary. Before he could speak, Norie Nakpodia beckoned for the man to sit. He brought him a serving of hot food, which the man ate quietly among racks of clothes available for free. Like his mother, Norie finds that helping others is like breathing. "I don't call them homeless; I call them unsheltered," he said as the man walked back onto Pine Street. "They have the same needs we do."

Nakpodia's philosophy has spread beyond her children. Strangers stop by with monetary and clothing donations. Some have signed on to help renovate the aging building, which dates to 1869, according to records Nakpodia found. Improvements are made a bit at a time, as money comes in. Shortly after she bought the building, she and supporters noticed a pervasive smoky odor. Church members pulled away cracked drywall panels to find soot-stained plywood behind the drywall, evidence of long-ago fire damage.

Another time, as helpers removed a drop ceiling, the remains of dead bats, birds, cats, and raccoons fell to the floor. Last year a group of retirees tackled the rear of the church, adding two bathrooms, two sinks, and a water heater. Last October, Nakpodia received a $500,000 grant from philanthropist Kym Rapier to restore the chapel and support her vision. Nakpodia was able to hire contractors to rewire half of the building and remove the gray clapboard exterior. She has plans for a new building behind the church called the Love Community Center, where her growing flock can shower, relax, and receive training and her counsel.

"I'm thankful there are so many who have helped me," Nakpodia said. "I couldn't do this all by myself."

Sounds of hammers and drill saws have replaced the echo of police sirens. The corner drug peddlers and prostitutes are all but gone. Green grass has sprouted at once-brown parched lots. On Saturdays Nakpodia and her volunteers host a food drive with Thrive Outreach, a nonprofit that offers breakfast and a bilingual prayer service behind the church.

After 1 p.m., the pastor and parishioners load up their vehicles with more than three hundred plates of hot food and drive along downtown streets, serving people who sleep under highway overpasses, inside entrances to cement storm drains, and atop metal drain grates.

The pastor sees a future where she owns a bus so volunteers can transport people to Redeemer's Praise for a meal, prayer, and promise of a new day.

"I believe in your lifetime to do the best that you can," Nakpodia said. "Our time here is so short. Whatever you can do to make this earth better, in your little corner, do it until it's time to depart. And do it wonderfully because you have finished your work."

Sam Greco's Life Began and Ended with Italian Saint

He was his mother's miracle. Elvira Battafarano Greco prayed to San Francesco di Paola for a son. After five miscarriages, she promised that if her prayers were answered, she'd dress the boy like a monk every Sunday for five years. She kept her promise.

Throughout his life, Sam J. Greco continued his mother's devotion to Saint Francis, the patron saint of Italians and Italian Americans. Greco died on November 14, 2023. He was eighty-two.

Last year Greco commissioned a six-foot-tall bronze sculpture of Saint Francis to replace a statue of Christopher Columbus that was removed from Piazza Italia Park in July 2020. Protests about the fifteenth-century explorer's treatment of Indigenous people led to the removal of monuments across the nation. On September 14, 2023, Greco stood with family, friends, parishioners, and dignitaries for the unveiling of the new statue. His gift to the city was his last civic act. Greco said the Italian community felt Saint Francis represented Italians and their ancestors' ocean crossings from Italy to America.

Greco was born in San Antonio on November 27, 1940, to Italian immigrant parents. Because his parents only spoke Italian, he reached out to a neighbor to teach him English. Salvatore Greco, a vegetable vendor, worked long hours to provide an education for his son. Family members said he laid some of the first red bricks at San

Francesco di Paola Catholic Church, a cultural center of the Italian community.

Sam Greco met his late wife, Kathy Fisher Greco, when they were sophomores. She attended Providence High School; he went to Central Catholic. Greco and his family dedicated the statue to her. He received a bachelor's degree in banking from Louisiana State University and a master's degree in finance from the University of Chicago. His family said that after a successful banking career he retired as the youngest bank president in the Lone Star state.

During their sixty-year marriage, the couple cofounded several companies, including Greco Construction, Pecan Valley Childcare Center, and S&K Management. Greco volunteered with several civic groups as director of the then Southside Chamber of Commerce, president of the Eastside Lions Club, and director of the Southeast Chamber of Commerce.

He passed the virtues of Saint Francis to his four children. They remembered their father as a storyteller and generous man whose home was open to those in need. They learned of their parents' good deeds—such as feeding the homeless and bringing them new coats when it was cold—from other people.

Darrell Greco said his father was known as the "Saint Francis baby." "I believe Saint Francis took care of him," said Sharon Pirro, Sam Greco's daughter. "I feel Saint Francis escorted him to heaven."

Brenda Greco Bowerman received phone calls from doctors who said her father touched their lives. "It says a lot about my dad," she said.

Diane Greco remembered her father as a man of peace who wanted his children to study and be aware of current affairs and the world around them.

Greco was the recipient of several prestigious honors. Giorgio Napolitano, the former president of Italy, bestowed Greco with the title Knight of the Order of the Star of Italian Solidarity. Condolences and remembrances came from near and far. Mauro Lorenzini, consulate general of Italy in Houston, thanked Greco for his "long commitment to the benefit of the Italian community in Texas."

Angela Lombardo, whom Greco counseled, remembered her friend's commitment to being an engine of change, a role he invited her and others to take up. Paolo Cristadoro, president of the Italian Society, said he sorely missed his friend and fellow society member. He recalled standing outside city hall with a smiling Greco and Linda Kohnen after receiving the final approval for the statue. He said during the eighteen-month process, Greco never lost focus on upholding the legacy of ancestors who settled San Antonio's Little Italy.

"It's a hard void to fill," Cristadoro said. "He was dedicated to getting the statue in place, not only for the community but his wife, whom he adored. He rallied everyone together. That was Sam."

Kohnen helped Greco with planning the two-day dedication event. She recalled her friend as a dynamic family man and advocate for the saint that was the church's namesake. "That was his grand finale," she said. "He made it happen, and it wasn't easy. He accomplished so much in his lifetime. We're all going to miss him terribly."

The retired businessman oversaw every detail of the statue's arrival in San Antonio. It was one of two sculptures he commissioned of the saint from Italian Canadian artist Antonio Caruso. The other statue stands in the seaside town of Paola in southern Italy. In July Greco joined society members for a dry run of the statue's placement at Piazza Italia, the downtown neighborhood settled by Italian families in the late 1800s. Before the dedication, Greco was hospitalized with ill health for five days. Society members said he insisted on being present for the event.

Greco led the procession of three hundred people from the church, pushed in a wheelchair by former mayor Henry Cisneros, to the park. He joined in tugging ropes that loosened the shroud from the statue, drawing applause from the crowd. "You did it," Cristadoro said as he leaned in to congratulate his friend.

It would be Greco's last display of devotion to the saint whose presence was woven throughout his family's lives. For Greco, it was a day that only happens once in a lifetime.

Faithful Sought a Miracle at a Tree

Faith seekers lined the curb of the East Side home. They came from across the city, the state, and as far away as the East Coast in search of one thing—a miracle. They sought cures for ailments, blindness, heart disease, and ravages of longevity. The object of their visit: an old red oak tree in the backyard that mysteriously spewed water. They called it the "weeping tree." Homeowner Lucille Pope said it was her "mystery tree."

In April 2006 Pope clung to the hope that her home was the site of miraculous healing water. She held on to that hope even after San Antonio Water System experts determined the tree's roots had tapped into the water line of a backyard shed.

The tree, more than a hundred years old, gurgled water for three months before the pilgrimages began. Pope called the Edwards Aquifer Authority, the Texas Forest Service, and nurseries, but the specialists couldn't give her an explanation. Before she received the utility's definitive answer, she just wanted to know if she had a "healing tree" or "blessed water." Pope said the pain in her swollen ankles went away when she soaked her feet in the water. "That's God's water," she said. "Nobody knows but God."

In early April 2006 Pope's son Lloyd saw a damp spot at the base of the tree trunk when he went to fill the water trough of his stepson's dog, Neno. Days later, water flowed to the ground from the other side of the trunk. Not long after, a continuous stream splattered against a parked 1980s white Cadillac.

People flocked to the site, as others did in the early 1990s after the reported sighting of tears wept by a statue of the saint named La Inmaculada at Our Lady of Guadalupe Church. There's a history of other reported sightings across the state. In 1998 a front yard statue of the Virgin Mary drew crowds to Corpus Christi. The homeowner said she saw the peeling plaster statue turn its head and take a small step in its alcove. In August 2007 worshippers at the Laredo Medical Center said they saw a consecrated host wafer that bore the image of Jesus. A Wilson County resident said that while making dinner, she discovered a tortilla with the image of the Virgin Mary on one side and Jesus on the other side.

Local academics said believers were seeking answers to ultimate questions. Jacob Friesenhahn, assistant professor of religious studies at Our Lady of the Lake University, said the image of purification excites the human religious imagination for some people. He said there was a time when settlers believed a spring of water was a sacred place—before aquifers took away the mystery of fresh water coming from the ground.

"I would break it down in how people have a craving for nature, not just the supernatural, but the supernatural that comes to us from nature," said Friesenhahn, forty-four, also program head for theology. "There's something kind of mystical about it and re-mystifying it." He said the concept of healing in water is an ancient narrative that crosses cultures. He noted how people fly to Lourdes, France, and line up for miles to soak in the waters.

In the Gospel of John, there's a healing pool where people crowd around to be first in the water. "There's something here where people are kind of craving something more mysterious," Friesenhahn said. "You could say modern society has kind of kicked out the supernatural, but people's hunger for it, it still pops up. There's this need maybe to find something extraordinary and kind of break us out of our routines."

Visitors to Pope's backyard held on to that belief even when told of a logical explanation. Before letting visitors in the yard, Lloyd Pope ensured that the faithful knew there was a scientific answer for the water that flowed from the tree like a half-running faucet. "I ain't with that superstitious stuff," he said as he caught water gurgling from the tree in a plastic gallon jug. "There's no crying Mary here."

When word spread of the unusual sight, crowds flocked to the home. They came from Dallas, Georgetown, and Laredo. The *San Antonio Express-News* did not publish the address, but people still tracked down the tree's location. The morning the story ran, it had 283 online hits; days later, the count had risen to 606,000 Google searches from China to New Zealand. *CNN*'s website ran a brief on the story. The Popes' landline rang with calls from almost every state in the nation—some callers asked about buying bottles of the mysterious water. Readers shared their opinions. Some questioned the eyebrow-raising sight and why God would present a watering tree during a drought. Another person supported those who had faith in miracles.

Lloyd Pope warned visitors that the water tested positive for chlorine residue. They still sipped the cool liquid pooled in cupped hands. They trickled it upon their faces. They held hands and prayed in hushed tones beneath the oak's sprawling branches.

Within weeks, the furor died down. The Popes no longer live at the home. Many of their neighbors who witnessed the scene have moved away or passed on. But Leonard Longoria, who lives a block away, knows the tale of the weeping tree. He wasn't around at the time, but his late mother-in-law, Rosa Valdez, told him about the spectacle that captured the attention of the city, state, and nation.

Valdez said everyone thought it was a miracle from God, but Longoria suspected something else. "I've seen it on our ranch," he said, at his front yard fence. "Tree roots tap into a water pipe and over time pressure builds and bursts through a hollowed-out part of the trunk."

Unlike those occurrences that seem normal in rural areas, the sight of water bubbling from a tree still has a place in San Antonio lore. Since then, the house has been renovated. New fabricated siding has replaced old wood panels. Any remnant of the home's past is covered, a sign of gentrification spreading across the once heavily populated African American community. One thing hasn't changed—the tree still stands.

THE UNSUNG

Ageless Dynamo Advocates for Area Seniors

For thirty years, Doris Griffin has fought for seniors to receive the dignity and respect she believes is often lacking. She's spoken on their behalf as a nine-term member of the Texas Silver-Haired Legislature at the state capitol in Austin. She's lobbied for better services, including transportation and nutrition, in government offices and corporate boardrooms. She has personally reaffirmed her support in the living rooms of seniors who greatly appreciated her home visits.

During the months since the novel coronavirus pandemic erupted, the safety and well-being of seniors are on Griffin's mind more than ever. Recently she's partnered with Dr. George Rapier III, founder of WellMed and chair of the WellMed Charitable Foundation, on an awareness campaign. Their message for people sixty-five and older is similar to that for people of all ages: wear masks, wash hands, practice social distancing, and shelter at home. But the message is tailored specifically for the needs of their audience.

The ageless dynamo insists that elders not be dismissed or spoken down to but venerated in these days of social isolation. "We want to show them that they are relevant," Griffin, eighty-nine, said at her North Side home. "We want to show them that they were born to be someone."

For more than twenty years, Griffin served as executive director of Jefferson Outreach for Seniors, which provided transportation for homebound seniors, mobile meals, a thrift shop, and grocery delivery services. She cochaired the City/County Joint Commission on Elderly Affairs and was part of a senior transportation coalition for quadrants of San Antonio.

In January 2015 the city and WellMed Charitable Foundation honored her work by opening the Doris Griffin Senior One Stop Center. Before the pandemic forced restrictions on visits at the center, the lively, ever-smiling Griffin would regularly stop by to talk to members who rushed toward her when they heard the tap-tap-tap of her heels and saw the bright colors of her grand outfits.

Widely known as a role model for seniors, Griffin is also known for always being fashionably dressed and for her signature high-heeled shoes. She is proud of the morals that are her foundation, and which she says originated with her family in America's heartland. Her moral code made her strong, she says, and gives her the ability to continue her work as she approaches her ninth decade. Age is just a number.

One of four children, Griffin grew up in Gobbler's Knob, a hamlet near Mount Washington, Ohio. She was in the fourth grade when her family moved from a one-bedroom home into a two-story home with a wraparound porch. As the American military fought in World War II against the Axis powers, her parents Clyde and Beulah Money taught her to revere the Lord and speak on behalf of others in need. They taught her about empathy in the fifteen-house community where neighbors spoke every day and could disagree without losing respect for one another. She recalled the day her father called her by her nickname and said, "Dode, whatever you ask of anyone else, make sure it's something you would do yourself."

"He taught me that you don't find happiness in money or fame," Griffin said, "but inside of yourself. You have to find something inside to keep yourself going."

She dreamed of singing with a big band, like Doris Day was doing with Les Brown and His Band of Renown. By the age of seventeen she had changed her name to Dixie West and was leading a band that played ballrooms and country clubs. Her burgeoning singing career was cut short two years later in 1949, however, when she married George Griffin, an airman who had served in World War II and opted to make the military a career. His duty assignments took them and their three children around the world to the Azores, Libya, Germany, and Alaska. During their travels, they made friends with families from different backgrounds, all drawn together by the same common needs. Her husband, a quiet man, put her in the spotlight during their fifty-seven years of marriage. After twenty-six and a half years in the air force, he retired as a chief master sergeant and settled his family in San Antonio.

"He was an amazing man," Griffin said. "Everybody loved my husband."

He supported his wife as a computer operator and lead volunteer at Jefferson Outreach. The couple and their daughter, Joy Martinez, joined other volunteers in visiting seniors they considered family, with the outreach programs. They delivered groceries and meals and took turns driving seniors to doctor appointments. They listened to the clients, who were often alone and looked forward to their home visits.

For Griffin it was a chance to see the elders face to face, offer emotional support, and check on their well-being. And it was a chance to treat people with dignity, just as her mother and father had taught her. Years later she and her family offered that same grace to her parents in their last days. She recalls brushing her father's hair, singing his favorite hymns, and telling him she loved him. Griffin said the same words to her mother, who was immobilized by a stroke. "If you can hear me, look at me," she remembers telling her mother, still moved by the memory. Minutes later, her mother turned her head and looked at Griffin. "That was a gift that God gave to me," she said.

In 2007, when Griffin's husband fell ill and his time grew short,

Griffin and her family surrounded him and said their last goodbyes. She said the words of love weren't any different than what they had said to him all of their lives. In these uncertain times of COVID-19, the advocate encourages everyone to express their feelings to elders now and not wait until it's possibly too late.

"People should say those things while they can," Griffin said. "You never know what's going to happen. Let them know how you feel and really take the time in your busy day to let people know what you think about them."

Eighty Years Strong

Nino Flores wields the wide steering wheel of his twenty-five-thousand-pound sanitation truck along San Antonio streets with a firm, two-handed grip. Coworkers wave and nod with respect as truck no. 2998 rumbles into softball parks and senior center parking lots. Flores climbs down from the cab at each stop, grabbing bags of trash and slinging them into the rear compactor as if tossing logs onto a fire. He pushes a baton-sized handle that sends a slab of metal scooping up waste and grinding it. Back in the cab, he turns on the air conditioner, and the sweet-sour smell of smashed food, tree limbs, and rubbish fills the cab with nary a sniff from Flores.

After twenty-seven years working with the San Antonio Parks and Recreation Department as a garbage collection truck driver, there's little about his job that bothers him. The only thing that strikes a nerve is if someone asks when he's going to retire. Many people have asked him that question over the past few years, more so since he recently turned eighty. "I'll keep working as long as I can keep walking or someone else retires me," Flores said, jabbing his index finger to the sky. "Instead of going up [in years], I'm going down."

Patricia Olivo, forty-five, worked beside Flores for eight years before transferring to work with the city's community initiatives. During their runs, Flores worked as hard as any young man, she said. “It was wonderful working with him. He’s a strong man for his age. He makes you laugh.”

After he’s done for the day, Flores heads home, where he lives alone. He’s been divorced for forty-two years. He spends much of his time with his three children. They’ve all pleaded with him to retire and rest. He says he doesn’t know how, convinced he would be bored if he had to sit at home. And he thinks a lot of health issues could creep up on him if he doesn’t stay busy. By 9 p.m. he’s asleep. He rises early, downing a cup of coffee before heading to work at 6:45 a.m. Living during the Depression taught Flores the importance of work. Since age seventeen, he’s sought any job he could land without a high school diploma. In a family of ten children, everyone had to do his or her share to survive, and Flores never had the opportunity for an education. He has stayed longer at the parks department than several coworkers who started at the same time as him. They’ve all retired.

So Flores’s path is a solitary one. But his coworkers treat him with reverence. Some even take his advice about life, and that brings a slight smile to his weathered face. He’s content working where the duties haven’t changed, people don’t hassle him, and he just does his job. A job, Flores said, that will be his last.

Flores worked for the department until he was eighty-six. He passed away in 2020.

Octogenarian Offers Inspections and Inspiration

The lean, eighty-five-year-old man is never far from fond memories of a life well lived. Those moments in time are frozen in photos nailed to the wall of his business—John's Inspection Station on South Flores Street. Customers see him in the early 1960s, sans shirt, striking a muscleman pose with bulging biceps as big as footballs. There's a photo of bodybuilder and actor Lou Ferrigno of *The Incredible Hulk* towering over him at a Traders Village event. And there's a framed, autographed eight-by-ten glossy of Jack LaLanne, the "Godfather of Modern Fitness," flexing his physique in his iconic jumpsuit.

The images map the octogenarian's rise as a disciple of physical fitness. His story starts at Burbank High School during the 1950s, when he envisioned one day being chiseled like body-building icon Eugen Sandow. John Ellis was a hundred-pound, sixteen-year-old when young men with slicked-back hair sang doo-wop from street corners into the night. Lifting weights with friends became his favorite pastime. Though his pals outweighed and towered over his five-foot-two-inch frame, size didn't matter to Ellis. What mattered was excelling at a pastime decided by something he had an endless supply of—determination. "I knew I was going to be a little guy," Ellis said, "but I was going to be the best little guy I could be."

He shares his story with clients in the dusty white cinderblock building with "John's Inspection" painted in red letters over the entrance. Customers get more than vehicles inspected in the bay; they also get inspiring life and spiritual tips from Ellis.

Recently he greeted drivers awaiting their check clad in a white short-sleeved shirt, gray sweatpants, and a black army baseball cap pressed upon wisps of gray hair.

"Hey, how are you doing?" he asks clients. They leave with "Thank you" and "God bless you." Before they leave, Ellis hands them a business card. On the back are three images of him in his twenties, flexing his herculean frame that won prizes and acclaim. His motto is "You come in as a customer. You leave as a friend."

For the past twenty years the army veteran has run the location just down the hill from his alma mater. Ellis started the business after he retired from twenty-five years of civil service at Randolph Air Force Base. A symbol of his faith is a plastic white crucifix dangling on his wall from strings of fiesta flowers inches from an image of Jesus with a glowing halo. High above it is a black-and-white photo of a young Ellis and his wife, Mary Ann.

He fell hard for her at first glance. They married three months after he walked her home from Sommers Drug Store on Nogalitos Street. The couple raised six children: three boys and three girls. A religious woman, Mary Ann Ellis died ten years ago, but she's always on his mind. He calls his wife of fifty-three years his "Earth Angel," the title of his favorite 1950s song. "It hurts every day," Ellis said as he lowered his head and took a breath. "Oh my God, I think of her every day."

Since 2007 his daughter Jennifer Ellis, forty-five, has worked at the station, inspecting vehicles and tending to technical tasks as he offers customers one-on-one attention. She recalled how teens who lift weights after school are intrigued by her father and the muscle man photos from his youth. "He's a true inspiration to anyone who meets him," she said. "Young people are influenced by him. I call him a living legend."

The old building, once a gas station and lounge, is a hub for many South Side residents, some of whom frequented Ellis's gyms. Longtime customer Danny Aguilar, fifty-one, has known Ellis and his family since he was eleven years old. He said stopping at the station is more than business—it's like visiting family. "He's from around here, which is where we're from," Aguilar said, from his car's rolled-down window. "So we try to keep it local as much as possible."

Today Ellis and his family are preparing for the grand opening of John's Gym in a room behind the bay. Ellis and his son Michael, forty-three, are providing a free workout space for neighborhood kids and athletes at his alma mater. The weight room is filled with benches, weights, and equipment donated by supporters and local gyms. "It's about love—that's what God is," Michael Ellis said of the space his family dedicated to fellowship and faith. "He has a heart of forgiveness and giving people a chance."

Ellis hopes to help youngsters get in shape, like he did as a teen pumping iron in his backyard. Unlike the free weights at his new gym, the dumbbells he lifted were coffee cans filled with concrete and ninety-pound cinderblocks. In his heyday, Ellis said he could bench press three hundred pounds. Ellis acknowledged he's a sliver of his once statuesque stature, when his back muscles fanned out wide as a manta ray's wingspan. Last week doctors put a pacemaker in his chest. Nine years ago Ellis had a quadruple-bypass operation. The surgeries sidelined him a bit, but he's never quit, passing his passion to his sons and grandsons. He lamented that over the years, friends he once lifted weights with have passed away. "They're gone," he said, "and I'm still here for some reason."

Ellis has devoted his remaining years to sharing the gospel about health and physical fitness. The days of powerlifting are behind him. These are days of moderate and light twice-a-week workouts at a TruFit Athletic Club on Southwest Military. And these are times when Ellis treats customers to his first love—singing songs from the 1950s—the theme music of his life. When he belts out a tune, his strong, stirring voice echoes around his bare-walled room set up for fitness and faith. Recently Ellis stood between the workstations, lifted his head, and sang a 1950s standard, "Angels in the Sky."

With arms open wide, he crooned of a heavenly place where he'd be seen and heard in the great beyond.

Long Legacy of Labor

On November 22, 1963, more than sixty men, women, and children lined a cold field southeast of San Angelo, stuffing tufts of cotton into sacks slung over their shoulders. The migrant farmworkers were in their fifth hour of work when their foreman arrived with devastating news: President John F. Kennedy had been assassinated. He said the nation was in mourning; they'd only have to work half a day.

Alfonso Morales stepped forward and spoke for the workers. "We're very sorry, we respected the president, and we feel very bad," he said. "But we have to keep working to make a living."

The workers knelt and said a prayer for the slain leader. Then they returned to picking cotton. On Monday the country celebrates Labor Day, a holiday the Morales clan and millions of other families rarely stopped work to celebrate. Morales's work history spans more than seventy years, from sharecropping and working cotton fields across Texas to tending to the lawns of attorneys and doctors in Alamo Heights. In early August he turned one hundred. His seven children and their families celebrated his birthday at his small South Side home with his wife, Rosa, ninety-five, who worked twelve-hour days beside him.

Recently Morales laid on his bed, resting his sore back, as Tejano songs played from an old tabletop radio. His daughters, Bernice Fernandez, seventy-seven; Terry Lopez, sixty; and Hortense de la

Rosa, sixty-nine, talked about how years of stooping over and picking crops had led to his bad back. "It was hard work, but I had to do it," Morales said through de la Rosa, who translated for him. "I always had to keep going. I had to feed my family."

"I relied a lot on my religion," he said. "I'm very thankful to God."

Two of Morales's children were already working with him during the early years of the Bracero Program that allowed Mexican nationals to work temporary agriculture jobs from 1942 to 1964. An overwhelming number of migrants across the nation are still of Mexican descent, said Patricia Sánchez, associate professor of bicultural-bilingual studies at the University of Texas at San Antonio. The work was hard, she said, without adequate breaks and with travels through small towns where they faced discrimination. She said workers still face the same conditions but do their jobs with pride in hopes of a better life for their children.

That was the sentiment of workers Sánchez said she interviewed for the documentary *Labors of Life, Labores de la Vida: Voices of Tejano Migrant Farm Workers*. "They're our unsung heroes," she said. "People always refer to Midwest farmers as salt of the earth. I think the nation should include these migrant workers who have done so much to put food on our tables."

Morales was born in Medina County, where he took up the work of his father. He met Rosa on a farm in La Coste. She fell for him when she realized he wasn't like other suitors; he talked about the world beyond the fields. They married in 1935 at Saint Alfonso's Catholic Church. He was twenty-two; she was seventeen. They raised three boys and four girls, and they worked mostly in Texas. The kids went to school from 7 a.m. to noon and then headed to work. Morales bought their two-room home, near Somerset Road, in 1953 when the area was full of trees and open fields. The kitchen served as a bedroom for Morales and his wife; the seven children slept in the other room.

In 1963 landscaping became Morales's source of income. His

clientele included judges, doctors, and lawyers, about a dozen customers a week. The five oldest siblings helped Morales so the two youngest children could concentrate on their studies. "They sacrificed a lot to put me and my sister [de la Rosa] through school," said Lopez, Morales's youngest daughter. "Mom and Dad kept us in line and showered us with a lot of love."

Morales worked until he was ninety. His customers still check on him. On August 4, more than fifty members of his family surrounded him in his bedroom as his daughters presented him with a hundredth-year birthday cake.

Joseph Garcia stood near a corner shrine, crowded with porcelain figures of saints, as his grandfather blew out his candles. He said Morales taught him lessons he still lives by. "It was instilled in all of us. You're supposed to be the best," he said. "That was our work ethic. It's all a trickle-down thing."

The family surprised Morales and hired mariachi trio La Alegria Tejana, who serenaded him with songs he'd sung in the fields. He smiled and, like a priest bestowing a blessing, raised his hand, leathery and rough from a life of hard labor, and marked time with the music.

Dressmaker Makes San Antonio Sparkle

Jackie Onassis black-framed glasses. Coiffed hair swept up with a flourish. Her attire, never off the cuff, is a study of style, class, and 1960s haute couture. Lucia Lozano stays ready for her close-up. The ninety-one-year-old dressmaker and designer makes alterations to a roster of private clients' clothes in a North Central home as exquisite as her fashion designs. Red drapery adorns pink walls. A white baby grand piano sits near porcelain statues perched upon a mantelpiece. Flecks of light reflect off crystal candelabras and a high-hanging chandelier.

Lozano is thankful for her clientele, which includes well-known San Antonian Mary Alice Cisneros, who beams in a framed portrait in the seamstress's studio. She's "Lucy" to her clients, drawn to her by word of mouth. As she does in life, Lozano doesn't hold back from offering her opinion about clients' clothing choices. "You tell me what you want, and it's done," Lozano said. "You're going to wear it—I'm not. I never push people on things like that."

Recently, former *San Antonio Express-News* reporter Elizabeth Allen stopped by for an emergency dress alteration. Fading sunlight cast a glow upon Lozano's work studio, where photos, pin cushions, and spools of thread lined the walls. After Allen slipped on a black lace dress, Lozano examined how the fabric fell on her form. The solution—take the sleek material in by hand and make it tighter for a better fit.

"That's why I come to you," Allen said.

"Yes," Lozano said, "I'm the saver."

Allen is director of external communications at University Health. She met Lozano through good friends in her neighborhood, joining the dressmaker's tight-knit circle. "She consented to be my friend," Allen said. "It's a wonderful thing to know a person like her. She's a treasure."

Days before the dress consult, Lozano shared her creations with Allen and visitors. The fashionista held up a dress she waited several years to complete—she had to find the perfect orange sequins. She revealed her version of the classic LBD (little black dress). Many garments were adorned with her trademark floral patterns that sparkled and shined. "They don't make these anymore," she said. "But I do. When you make an entrance, everyone has to see you."

Her grandmother, a midwife, delivered her at the family home in New Braunfels. Though her family wasn't rich, she was raised to believe that wasn't a reason not to look presentable in public. Lozano's penchant for fashion began when her mother would dress her like Shirley Temple, the popular child actress of the 1930s. At the same time, her mother taught her and her sister, Juanita, to play the guitar. By 1944, they were playing and singing like their idol Lydia Mendoza, known as "La Alondra de la Frontera" (Lark of the Border). A high point of their career was playing with Mendoza at a concert in Corpus Christi.

Lozano was young when her mother taught her the basics of dressmaking. By her teen years, sewing and singing were stitched into her life. The oldest of seven children, Lozano didn't finish high school. Instead she chose to work and earn money to sew nice clothes like the stars on the silver screen. Backed by sharply dressed musicians, she sang with her two sisters on weekends as the Carmona Sisters.

Her wages went to her mother, and she was always home at the Alazán Courts before the city's 10 p.m. curfew. As the trio married and started families, Lozano went solo. She sang at nightclubs with names like Little Joe's, El Ranchito, and La Conga.

She met her husband of fifty-nine years, Ruben Lozano, in 1948 after he emigrated from Monterrey, Mexico, to the United States. She fell in love with the young man with a pencil-thin mustache and passion for life. The couple was a fixture at formal black-tie affairs where bow ties were given to men without one. Older photos show Lozano singing on a bandstand, maracas in hand, as her husband, in a natty suit, swings on the dance floor. Black and white snapshots show Lozano at swank affairs like the Black and White Ball, with female friends draped in glittering gowns she designed and sewed.

The decades whirled by with the couple waltzing across dance floors, hand in hand. They celebrated their fiftieth anniversary with a vacation in Europe. They had one child, Ruben Roland Lozano, a graduate of computer science at Trinity University. In 1989, when Roland's health was failing, the couple flew to San Francisco to care for him. Lozano would stay up late with him, talking about movies and food they both enjoyed. Bonding with her son as an adult remains a precious memory. Roland died nine months later. Lozano mourned him for a year and a half. "I cried until I had no more tears," she said. "It was the hardest thing. I understand very well when someone loses a child."

Hosting neighborhood parties lifted away her grief. The number of friends attending rose from several to 119 guests at one point. The couple's backyard parties grew into mini galas Lozano planned with precision, especially her Fourth of July extravaganza.

Each soiree takes a month to prepare. Lozano orchestrates everything, from seating arrangements, menus, and invitations to selecting just the right china. It's not work, she said—it's all for her guests' enjoyment. For the past eleven years, she's hosted the gatherings alone. Her husband and dancing partner died on Father's Day in 2010. Lozano continues doing everything they did together—the gatherings keep her going. "I don't desire [anything] any more," she said. "I keep on working. I'm still living; I'm not dead yet."

She has no regrets. There are still dresses to create, alterations to make, and parties to plan. Occasionally she will turn back the years to nights when she graced bandstands in gowns she'd labored on for days. And, as she once serenaded crowds in nightclubs, she'll turn to the guests who give her joy, open her arms, and sing.

Lozano passed away July 6, 2023. She was ninety-two.

Dare Helps Retiree Find Calling

It started with a dare. Fifteen years ago, George Hookings accepted a challenge from his daughter Stephanie at a club on San Pedro Avenue. His wife, Carole, and their three daughters often dared him at karaoke bars to go up and sing like he did at home. For more than forty years Hookings had sung a variety of songs with his wife's family, who played musical instruments during get-togethers.

His selection that night: "Mack the Knife." Hookings was petrified, but the crowd loved him. Afterward people complimented him and requested other songs.

Today the bespectacled man with pepper gray hair is a professional crooner. Dressed in black semiformal wear, accented with a tie, he starts his show in the fading, golden light of day. He grasps a silver microphone and dips the mic stand forward. Then he gazes across the dining room, belting out melodies from yesteryear's hit parade.

Hookings's velvet voice keeps songs of days gone by alive four nights a week at Pompeii Italian Grill on Nacogdoches Road. Hookings, one of San Antonio's last restaurant singers, is upholding a long-honored tradition. He's had a standing residency at the Northeast Side restaurant for the past four years. The only time he was sidelined from performing was during the pandemic.

"The only thing I have is my voice," Hookings, sixty-eight, said.

"Whether it's three tables or thirty tables, I will do the songs with the same enthusiasm. You always give 110 percent."

He grew up in Jersey City, New Jersey, in the era of fin-tail cars and rabbit-ear TV antennas wrapped in aluminum foil. He was captivated by crooners who sang songs such as "April in Paris" and "I Left My Heart in San Francisco." His love for singing comes from his mother, who he sang with in the car and duetted with on songs like "Moonlight Bay" at their weekend home at Upper Greenwood Lake. His work ethic comes from his father, a bus driver who worked two four-hour shifts each day.

Hookings worked at a UPS call center in Secaucus, New Jersey, for ten years before a transfer in 1995 brought him and his family to San Antonio. After twenty-seven years he retired from the company. Idle time replaced workdays, and he was in need of a busy pastime. His idea of a bucket list is fronting a big band, singing songs made famous by "BTF." The acronym doesn't stand for a boy band but rather iconic singers Bobby Darin, Tony Bennett, and Frank Sinatra. "They have a plethora of songs to choose from," Hookings said.

The crooner's song styling complements the rustic, warm ambiance at Pompeii, where waiters and waitresses serve in time with the music. Hookings recalled when a woman requested a version of "The Green, Green Grass of Home" by Tom Jones, a song he was semi-familiar with. After his rendition, she hugged and thanked him for lifting the spirits of her ninety-one-year-old father by singing his favorite song.

Diners Julia and Michael Drapala, both forty, were impressed by the singer's selections. They favor old songs laced with swirling strings that sweep listeners away to dimly lit corners for two. Michael Drapala said Hookings's voice reminded him of stories his nana told of seeing a young Frank Sinatra sing at quarter shows in the 1940s. The couple had one song request: Sinatra's "My Way." "People like him," said Rosa Borrego, fifty-five, Pompeii assistant manager. "A lot of people come back because of him. He connects with them."

Often Hookings muses about an imaginary venue in another time and place. He sees himself backed by an orchestra or top high school musicians at an audience-filled symphony hall, performing a Bobby, Tony, and Frank show.

The crooner walks on stage and picks up a baton. He's ready to wave the musicians into a song until the orchestra leader points him offstage. Hookings's job, the maestro says, is to sing. And that's his plan, until the day he packs up his one-man band and takes his last curtain call.

Panchos and Gringos Customers Step Up

Customers at a Dignowity Hill diner are so dedicated to the eatery that they're volunteering to keep the place running after one of the most challenging years for restaurants in recent history. The city's pandemic safety protocols caused Sergio Calderon, owner of Panchos and Gringos, to shut down the restaurant at Nolan and Pine Streets for weeks in 2020. When Calderon reopened, he set up curbside service. He later opened for dining inside. But several employees didn't return, including a longtime waitress who left to care for an ailing relative.

The restaurateur isn't 100 percent healthy himself. He has an injured knee and had a heart attack two months ago. Like many restaurant owners, Calderon has struggled to make the profits he once did before the spread of the coronavirus. More than 110,000 eateries and drinking locations nationwide closed temporarily or for good in 2020, according to a report from the National Restaurant Association. At the height of the closures an estimated eight million workers were furloughed or laid off. In late July Calderon had to pick up the slack. And on crowded days he had to do the unthinkable: turn diners away.

Calderon's fortunes began to turn around a few weeks ago when customer Alyson Fitzpatrick learned that on top of his grilling duties, Calderon had to help his three-member staff clean tables, serve customers, and work the cash register. Fitzpatrick, a school psychologist with East Central Independent School District, volunteered to help despite not having waitress or cash register experience. Calderon, sixty-four, chalked up her offer as a well-meaning gesture. But one Sunday, Fitzpatrick, thirty-three, returned at 8 a.m. After a crash course on waiting tables, she pitched in to lessen the load that had weighed upon Calderon for months.

The diner, open from 8 a.m. to 2 p.m. Tuesday through Sunday, has a clientele that is a mix of East Side residents, city employees, businesspeople, and customers who have frequented the restaurant since it opened nine years ago. It's a place where Calderon whips up special dishes for regulars. He pulls up a chair to see how diners are faring and to serve up bits of wisdom gleaned from his grandfather Eduardo Calderon Espinoza, a former general in the Mexican army. He's even named specials after loyal customers and set up a reserved table and corner for blues musician Curley Mays, who stops by every morning. "My customers are like family," Calderon said as the sound of chattering patrons and clattering dishes filled the dining room.

Fitzpatrick returned last weekend with coworker Ernest Ramos, thirty-eight, who cleared tables during his first volunteer shift. When Fitzpatrick told him how she spent her Sunday, he signed on to the team. "I've definitely never seen anything like this," Ramos said. "I guess I've always kind of saw that kind of thing in a movie. It's the kind of a story you hear or read about, but you've never been a part of it."

Other surprises awaited Calderon. One customer learned about the extra helpers and offered to buy their lunch. Calderon thanked the man and said the restaurant would provide their meals. He suggested the customer leave a tip for the volunteers instead. Minutes later Fitzpatrick beckoned Calderon to the tablet cash register. "Sergio," Fitzpatrick said, "look at this tip."

"Wow," Calderon said, with a quick glance. "A $50 tip!"

"No," she said, "look again."

Calderon's eyes widened. The customer had left a $500 tip. "I've never seen that before in my life," he said, days later. "I've been doing this for forty-five years, and this was unreal for me, completely unreal. I really appreciate what they did. This shows how San Antonio people are, and I love it."

The diners' selfless streak continued. A woman at a table of eight pitched in and served her party. They left a $300 tip. A diner at table sixteen listened to Calderon's story with tear-filled eyes. She slid a $100 bill under her plate. At the end of that workday Calderon was stunned by the $900 in tips that customers had left. He said tips might total $150 on an average day. He split the money with Fitzpatrick, who has texted friends to come out and support Calderon.

"We didn't want him to close; we love his food," she said, during a break. "We can give back and help out. The idea was for people to come here and want to work. We want to get the word out."

Fitzpatrick and Ramos plan to keep helping out on weekends and hope there's an upswing of fortune for the owner of Panchos and Gringos. That's the same sentiment of Cody Crislip, twenty-six, who has been a customer for the past two years.

The owner of Small Hamster Hosting said he hopes the COVID-19 era ends soon and that there are better days for Calderon and scores of businesspeople. "Sergio is really a good guy," Crislip said. "He's the sunshine in our day."

Helping Thirsty MLK Marchers Is Her Mission

It is her ministry. For the past thirteen years, Janice Brock has waded into the tide of marchers at San Antonio's Martin Luther King Jr. March for one reason—to offer bottled water to the tired and thirsty. Brock and her supporters arrive on the East Side by 8:45 a.m. with carloads of water. They set up before authorities close the street to traffic on the 2.75-mile route along MLK Drive. When the wave approaches, they grab armfuls of bottles from plastic bins.

The procession, thick with banners and signs for unity, will stall at the Interstate 10 underpass. That's when Brock and her team walk through the crowd and hand out water at one of the nation's largest MLK marches. "Whoever is out there, we tell them thank you for marching," said Brock, sixty-one. "And then go back and get more. It's humbling that God allows me to do this."

Brock is one of the unsung who offers water to the masses without fanfare. The teachings of the late civil rights leader inspire her humanitarian cause. A self-described child of the 1960s, she fondly remembers King's campaign for equality and peace during the turbulent era. "We need to teach kids about being part of something bigger than themselves," she said. "And show respect for those who fought so we could have the freedoms that we have. We need to keep it going and pass it on."

Years ago she marched with her sons, Fredricc and Virgil Jr., when they were small. It was her way of teaching the youngsters about giving back to their community and remembering where they came from. They walked from their house at the corner of Olive and Dawson Streets to the MLK Plaza at Houston and New Braunfels, the former site of the MLK march commemoration ceremony. A back injury ended her days in the procession.

"I was crushed when I couldn't march any more," Brock said. "I feel like the people are marching not only for me, but me and everyone who can't physically march anymore."

Brock relied on her faith for an answer. She said prayer offered an alternative—hand out water at the march. She used her own money to get started. Friends and family donated whatever they could. Brock started with 325 bottles; her supply was gone within seconds. She didn't like telling people she was out of water.

The next year she had some 650 bottles, and the number has grown ever since. Brock and her team hand out water at Badger Street and MLK Drive, outside the house where her mother once lived. The residents, Daniel Simmons, eighty-four, and his family, welcomed Brock when she asked if her team could use their front yard as their base. The Simmonses support Brock's initiative, offering the team a place to rest, recoup, and sit for a while. "She does a great job and deserves all of the kudos," Simmons said. "We're glad she does it on our property."

The army Vietnam veteran said he'll be proudly wearing his 82nd Airborne cap on his porch, waving to the passing crowd.

"They've been so gracious to allow me every year to hand out water," Brock said. "It's truly appreciated."

Her outreach was suspended for three years by COVID-19 and emergency surgery. This year she had to rush and stock up—she learned of the in-person march only two weeks ago. Her daughter-in-law Kan'Dace Brock put out a call to her line sisters of Delta Sigma Theta Sorority, who responded with dozens of donations. Brock calls her "daughter-in-love."

A week before the march, Brock bought 1,280 bottles of water. Without a storage shed, she's had to improvise. Last week thirty-two cases were stacked behind two chaise lounges in her living room. She hopes one day that she'll be blessed to have a unit to collect water months ahead of time. "I hope to do this as long as I can," she said. "My goal is that each marcher has a bottle of water."

Today she'll be with her son Fredricc and her daughter-in-law. She'll also work beside an older grandchild, who she calls one of her original worker bees. Brock first brought her to the route when she was four. She wants her grandchild to learn to respect people whose sacrifice made their lives better and offer service to others—the same principles she taught her sons. They'll serve marchers from all walks of life. Parents carrying children. The old and young. Different races, arm in arm. Everyday people side by side with those who make headlines.

"To hear people say, 'Someone thought of me and handed me a bottle of water,' that to me is priceless," Brock said. "This is the one day that everyone seems to be of one accord. It's more than handing out water. It's my prayer and hope that people will keep a dialogue with each other. It's awesome to see."

San Antonio Native Scours Streets to Clean Windows

The wiry window washer apologized as he maneuvered around tourists on downtown sidewalks en route to his next job. With whispers of sorry disappearing behind him, Michael Anthony "Mike" Ruiz arrived at his destination, EHCÜ Public Relations on Broadway, his sweat-drenched shirt clinging to his lean frame.

He dunked his brush in the gray plastic bucket of water and swiftly lathered the surface with dripping suds that splattered across the pavement. Ruiz squeegeed away veils of dishwashing liquid with long, S-shaped strokes to reveal a crystal-clear view through the office window. He walked inside and leaned inches from the window to inspect the glass for any smudges or streaks. After getting his client's vote of approval, he grabbed his equipment and hustled outside past a chocolate shop and Thai restaurant, headed to his next job.

"This is how I live and make it through the day," said Ruiz, forty-seven. "It's my work. I've got to put food on the table."

For the past twenty-five years the San Antonio native has earned money for his wife and children by cleaning windows for an estimated seventy clients that have included Earl Abel's Restaurant, Cadillac Bar, and Paris Hatters. His current client list stretches from the city's center to strip malls in the suburbs. Depending on the number of windows, his pay ranges from $10 to $40 for one-story buildings in and around downtown. Some days he clears $200.

Other days not so much, barely earning enough for a fast-food meal for his family.

Ruiz said that during his career, he has worked with local companies such as Tracy Cleaning and Winco of South Texas, and in the past he's washed windows for businesses in and around downtown Fort Worth. His skill set includes power cleaning and power washing. He's also painted high-rise buildings.

He first worked with his father, Frank Ruiz, in the window-washing business. Two years ago he struck out to work for himself. Things were going well until his father died. He became depressed and stopped going to work. He lost his house and his car, temporarily rendering him and his family homeless.

Then he met Keith Witt, owner of Winco, Ruiz said, who believed in him and encouraged him to step out on faith. Witt, who has been in the Texas window cleaning business since 1979, uses his business to affect the lives of the less fortunate. He helped Ruiz's family when the window cleaner was jailed for fighting. Over the years Witt said he's hired Ruiz back several times as he has others just out of prison or recovering from addictions.

"We're a second chance company," he said. "All of us have to be humble. We don't look down on our nose at people. We need to look with deep respect. I love him and I hope the best for him."

Ruiz is the youngest of twelve children. He grew up on the South Side, working around town with his father, who always told him, "No window is going to beat you." He rises every day at 5 a.m. and says a prayer that begins, "Let me make it out there."

"I know God is there," Ruiz said. "God is good."

Then it's a bus ride from the West Side where his family lives to downtown, his main workplace. Ruiz starts by stopping at a parking garage to fill his bucket with water, then stirs in several drops of Dawn dish soap. The soapy water sloshes in the bucket as Ruiz scrambles from job to job, logging more than twenty miles a day on foot. He weaves like an NFL running back around tourists and downtown workers, hurrying to his next customer's shop, his baseball cap and T-shirt soon soaked with sweat, even on cold days.

All his equipment fits in his bucket: a squeegee, a bottle of soap, a brush, sponge, rags, and a razor blade to scrape away paint and debris. Ruiz said lugging the equipment in one-hundred-plus degree summer heat has resulted in him dropping from 200 pounds to 150. In the fall and winter he dresses warmly, but when it rains there's no need to worry about special gear because that's when the work washes away and he stays at home.

When artist and entrepreneur Gilbert Glaster had a shop downtown, he exclusively hired Ruiz. He said that before he met Ruiz, he had to come in early himself to clean smeared fingerprints off the windows. Then one day Ruiz arrived with equipment in hand. He introduced himself as the man on a mission to keep San Antonio clean.

"That's when I knew he was serious about his job," Glaster said. "There had been other guys, but they were trying to get small change. When Mike came around it was a big help."

Ruiz cleaned Glaster's windows for close to a year, arriving every day.

In the future Ruiz hopes to work on a high-rise building, as he has in the past. The job commands higher pay, but he can't afford the required insurance. For now he's a company of one, washing windows, painting, and doing odd jobs seven days a week. "I have faith," he said. "I'll be up there."

For Ruiz, this time of year is bittersweet. He misses his father, but he'll spend Christmas with family at his sister's home. It's also a time when business slows. The only upside to fewer hours is he'll have a chance to rest his throbbing feet. The downside this year is not having made enough money to buy gifts on his youngest son Damian's Christmas list.

"It'll be tough," Ruiz said. "But whatever he gets it'll be all right."

José Arias's Smooth Moves at Ninety-Two

Five hundred people packed the Lirico theater in Monterrey, Mexico, in 1935 to watch twenty couples compete for the title of best swing dancers. One of the contenders, seventeen-year-old José Arias moved like a matador. With a turn of his wrist he guided his partner, his suit flowing along the contours of his body. For years, Arias had studied the elegant moves of matinee idol Fred Astaire in dark movie houses. He practiced five hours a night, four nights a week, at La Playa, a club where patrons paid five cents for admission.

The roar of the crowd affirmed his hours of dedication. After three hours the pair was crowned king and queen of swing. When the judges presented him with his trophy, Arias handed it to his partner—his custom after each win. "Respect to a woman," he said, "was basic."

Arias, ninety-two, a retired tailor, owes his career to his love of dancing and the suits the dance masters wore while gliding across the floor. But as a young boy, he couldn't afford the caliber of suits Astaire wore. So he made his own ensembles. At age ten, he worked at tailor shops doing hems and alterations. Six years later he was sewing suits in his own tailor shop, supporting his mother and three sisters.

Recently, wearing a tan guayabera, brown pants, and closed-toe sandals, he explained his lifelong love of dance at the Morningside Ministries Senior Living Communities. Administrative assistant Millie Gonzales translated as Arias talked of the driving force behind his life as a tailor. Before he married, he had girlfriends who twirled their bodies and tilted their heads at his slightest touch. They instinctively knew when to arch their sleek backs that he supported with his palm. He later worked for a boss who sent him to his San Antonio shop, but not before asking him about his goals in life. Arias replied that he wanted a good education for his children, and to own a nice home and a convertible. The man said a simple tailor would never earn those things.

With the resolve that spun him on the dance floor, Arias worked at the man's San Antonio shop eighty hours a week for a year. He worked eleven years at Sugar Uniforms to provide for his wife, Santos; daughter, Martha A. Avila; and sons Francisco, Gerardo, Isidoro, Jose A. Arias, and Juan Rangel. Then he started his own business from home, sewing for Dillard's for three years and JC Penney for thirteen years. "He came and worked hard," said his son Jose. "You always felt it was his calling."

At age eighty-nine, Arias retired from sewing but not from his stylish moves. He remembered stopping at a West Side club in 1958, where pictures of the bartender dancing hung behind the bar. She was a former professional dancer, tall and thin, with short curly hair and olive skin. As he ordered a soda, she slid a quarter in the slot of the jukebox and pushed the button for "La Cumparsita," sung by Carlos Gardel.

"That's a very nice song," he said.

"Do you know how to dance?" she said.

"Yes, I know how to dance," he said, and showed her his winning bolero and tango.

Arias still practices, but his partner these days is a walker bearing his name in black marker on a white label. His wife of sixty-two years died a year ago. He lives alone in an apartment, light-years away from the crowd-packed ballrooms where women whispered "He's here" when he arrived in bright-colored suits.

He demonstrated his form to visitors, the same moves that led to agents asking him as a young man to tour South America, a request he turned down to stay with his family. Arias extended his arm for Gonzales to take his hand at an outside courtyard. He spun and twirled her in a pirouette against his waist. She held her chest as Arias smiled and complimented her.

"It made me realize I need to start dancing," Gonzales said. "It brought so many memories of my grandpa in Peru."

Arias is known to surprise the nurses with a quick tango at Morningside dances.

"The tango is like a poem," he said. "And I memorized the composition."

EVERYONE IN THE CEMETERY IS FAMILY

Freedman's Descendants Remember

Rufus Francis Jr. had mixed emotions about the thirty-five-mile drive from San Antonio to the old freedman enclave. The San Antonio resident was invited by his aunt, Betty Young, with whom he spent summers as a child in the small community. Francis was among more than sixty people who filled the pews last Sunday in the small country church built by former enslaved settlers. For Francis, forty-eight, it was a time of reverence and remembrance. Sitting with his fiancée, Josefina Khan, he enjoyed the family atmosphere of the service. Still, he also felt saddened, and afterward he paid his respects to family members buried at nearby Sweet Home Cemetery.

Descendants of African Americans who founded the Freedmen Community of Sweet Home southwest of Seguin recently returned for the 159th anniversary of Sweet Home Baptist Church, their ancestors' spiritual birthplace. They traveled in cars, trucks, and SUVs from San Antonio, Houston, and other cities across Texas to the Sunday service. The scattered motorcade rolled down two-lane Sweet Home Road for an afternoon of testimonies, praise, and gratitude.

Yvonda Quarles, chairwoman of the homecoming committee, said the anniversary is their biggest worship service of the year. "This was a blessing," said Quarles, fifty-eight. "Everyone comes back. It brings us all together. This is a day we can never take back but will always remember."

During the program, older deacons and the choirs sang spirituals first performed in the sanctuary by relatives passed on to glory. Young praise dancers drew parishioners to their feet. The pastors preached sermons that reminded the congregation of how far they've come on a path paved by their forebears' sacrifice.

Sweet Home was one of Guadalupe County's first Black communities, which include Capote, Jakes Colony, and Zion Hill. In 1870 Black residents made up 34 percent of the county population. By 1980 that number had dwindled to 6 percent. According to church history, the Reverend John Moses started the gatherings in 1864 in a brush arbor under an old oak tree in the settlement—it was called Elm Creek Baptist Church. In 1905 the church moved to its present site.

German immigrant and businessman William Stein donated three acres of land for a church and school. A year later a storm destroyed the building. The Reverend S. A. Pleasant led the rebuilding of the structure with master carpenter Henry Singletary and volunteers. In November 1953 the present sanctuary was built under the leadership of the late Reverend E. L. Roach, pastor of the church for forty-two years. "This building was built up by soldiers of the Lord," said Addison Shepherd from Antioch Missionary Baptist Church in San Antonio.

Afternoon sunlight streamed through green and yellow stained-glass windows, casting a glow upon parishioners and stylish church hats worn by two older women. Ongoing responses from parishioners echoed through the service to selections by the choir and organ played by the Reverend Vincent E. Jennings, pastor of the church.

"This is another day's journey, and I'm glad about it—aren't you glad?" he said, to a chorus of amens. "We are so glad to see all of you. It blesses our heart and graces our heart."

Jennings introduced guest speaker Rev. Jimmie Flakes from Second Baptist Church in Seguin, who spoke of the need for the congregation to keep moving forward. "A stagnant creek serves no purpose at all," Flakes said. "We need to take it to the next level."

Lynda Richardson looked around the sanctuary, pleased at seeing cousins and relatives she'd known all her life. She spent her childhood summers in the country with her aunt Leola Lee. Kerosene lamps lit the two-bedroom home. She helped with chores, shelling peas, shucking corn, and hauling water from a well. For years she used lessons learned in the settlement as a volunteer with neighborhood youth and owner of an adult care center. "We need to speak about our history," Richardson said. "We have a diamond that we keep from being put under a rock."

A church leader asked those born and raised in the settlement to stand. Applause welcomed a dozen women and men who stood, cousins or related in one way or another. After the service, they walked across the street for dinner in the historic one-story Sweet Home Vocational and Agricultural High School. The inscription on a Texas historical marker outside states that the school served Black students from 1924 to 1962. It was one of six schools in Guadalupe County paid for by philanthropist Julius Rosenwald to improve the quality of education for rural residents in the early twentieth century.

Singletary, the master carpenter, and church usher Jesse C. Ussery built the school with four primary classrooms, a library, and a kitchen. It's now owned by the church and used as a community center and fellowship hall.

Quarles and her sister, Yvette, helped their mother, Constance Quarles, eighty-nine, up the stairs of the schoolhouse. She was five when she first walked two and a half miles from her family farm to the school. Constance Quarles recalled one of their notable alumni, the late Reverend E. V. Hill, pastor of Mount Zion Missionary Baptist Church in Los Angeles and ally of Martin Luther King Jr. In 1973 Hill gave the invocation at President Richard Nixon's inauguration.

After the service Francis, the San Antonio resident, drove to the cemetery to pay his respects to his father and grandmother. He parked on a stretch of red dirt beyond white-tipped wildflowers that sprouted around brown grass. His fiancée sat on a bench as he walked to a row of family members' graves adorned with flowers by church members. He stopped and smoked a cigarillo before his father's grave. The headstone's engraving reads, "Rufus Knole Francis. Jan. 4, 1954–Dec. 8, 2017. In God's loving care."

Francis remembered how snow fell the night before his father died and phoned to say he loved him. A few plots down from his father's grave were the headstones of his grandmother, Sterlene McIntyre Francis, and his cousin Clarence Cunningham, who taught him how to ride horses.

"Everyone pretty much in the cemetery is family," he said.

Long Lost Stories of Black Enclaves

For years retired U.S. Air Force Major J. Michael Wright wondered why all the property in his Northeast Side subdivision had been developed except for a single acre-size lot, fenced in and packed with trees and thorny brush. As he walked his two children to Northern Hills Elementary School day after day, they watched the chaparral on the neglected plot next to the school grow to twice its original size. He joked with his kids that maybe it was a secret nuclear site. There were rumors it was a graveyard.

Eventually curiosity overcame him and he began researching. He found a map at the Bexar County tax assessor-collector's office that positively identified the lot as a cemetery. But whose was it? Why had it been abandoned? Were there still human remains there?

Wright's quest led him to archivist David Carlson of Bexar County's Spanish archives office. Carlson researched deeds and records for the area, including the late 1800s U.S. census, and found tantalizing clues that the cemetery might once have been part of a long-lost African American settlement connected to the community of Wetmore, northeast of what's now the San Antonio International Airport.

It was the start of a surprising journey that would uncover other African American enclaves in the area long lost to history and the families that established them: Hockley, Winters, and Griffin. As

Wright and Carlson continued their hunt in the early days, online and in person, they talked to former gravediggers, funeral home directors, genealogical societies, and state experts. And they found out about landscape architect Everett L. Fly, a San Antonio native nationally recognized for preserving historic sites across the nation. Wright emailed Fly a summary of the records he and Carlson had accumulated for more than a year.

"It was like an aha moment," Fly said. "There's more to this, just like I thought. I could tell there was some real substance to it, and it was authentic information." The locations verified that there were Black quadrants of the city, in that area. "I knew right away there should be something that could be done and addressed in a more formal way."

Fly secured a grant from the San Antonio Conservation Society for travel expenses, research, and reproduction copies. He enlisted help from the city's Office of Historic Preservation, and city archaeologist Kay Hindes and Austin architect Ellen Hunt joined the effort. Wright and Carlson continued their volunteer efforts, working with the professional team. It was painstaking work, because there was a dearth of official information.

Fly said some records kept on African Americans from that time listed only a first name and no information on where the person was born. Some African Americans took new names, which made it difficult to trace family connections. And in many cases, no records at all were kept about African Americans.

The team turned to oral histories and family stories. There the researchers were fortunate. They discovered numerous modern-day descendants of the three families who had kept cherished documents passed down from generation to generation—some tucked away in Bibles and shoe boxes dating to 1865 that yielded information not found in libraries or city archives.

Tales told from mother to daughter, father to son also helped to piece together this little-known part of San Antonio history. Fly found a key common factor in the Wetmore area settlements: they all were started by former slaves, finally freed on June 19, 1865, two and a half years after Abraham Lincoln signed the Emancipation Proclamation.

Descendants of the Winters family have a copy of the emancipation letter in which E. C. Alsbury freed their ancestor Robert "Bob" Winters from slavery. The short letter is written in longhand and has "San Antonio, Texas," and "July 1st, 1866," at the top. In the letter, Alsbury credited Winters for "faithful service" and gave him possession of two horses. Alsbury also helped Winters buy land, Fly said.

A treasure trove of information came from a handmade book and a nine-foot-long family tree produced by descendant Edward Winters, who spent years poring over deeds, treaties, archives, and other records and talking with now-deceased family members. The book helped Fly make more connections between the Winters and Griffin families.

Fly returned the favor, giving family members data he had uncovered that they hadn't known. For example, Robert Winters had one of the five Black cattle brands registered with Bexar County. Some were marked "COL" for colored. Fly also told the family that the emancipated Winters had dedicated land for a school, a church, and the cemetery, forming the traditional nucleus of the community.

The information was new but didn't surprise some family members. "We were civic, we were community, and we were spiritual," Kevin Winters said. "And we're still community-minded today."

Melanie Winters Brooks called the discoveries surreal. "When I was a young girl, I didn't appreciate the family unit for what I understand now," she said. "The civic duties and how they helped established the Black presence in this community for the time that they did and the progressiveness of this family is overwhelming."

Fly met with Brooks, Kevin Winters, and a dozen other Winters descendants at Brooks's home on the South Side last month. They gathered around Daniel Winters, eighty-three, the patriarch of the family. He was born in a house not far from Thousand Oaks Drive and Wetmore Road. He remembers walking with his parents to clean the Winters family cemetery, which was located near where a Jim's Restaurant now is, at Nacogdoches Road and Loop 1604. That cemetery no longer exists; the remains of the seventy-one people buried there were relocated in 1986 to the Holy Cross Cemetery.

Before Wright and Carlson met Fly, they made several visits to the overgrown lot they now know as the Hockley Cemetery. The retired major and the archivist slogged through calf-high grass on an easement to climb over the chain-link fence into the thorny chaparral, where they scoured for anything that might shed light on the area's history.

Crawling under a tree, Carlson found a chunk of stone with worn letters spelling "Green" carved into the surface that could have been a headstone. About the only other things they found were dozens of old baseballs, perhaps left by kids who hadn't dared venture into the darkness of the thick undergrowth.

As they continued to search through documents, Carlson found a drawing that showed 1.262 acres marked as a rectangle-shaped cemetery, abutted and bookended by houses, cul-de-sacs, and crosswalks near Uhr Lane and Higgins Road. Maps prepared by LostTexasRoads.com show survey lines of the graveyard from a 1908 Bexar County deed record matching the Bexar County Appraisal District Record of the property as "Lot P-99 (CEMETERY)." Bexar County archives showed that the property once was owned by Jane Warren, who was born in 1830 in Alabama. By 1847 she was living in Hays County. In 1908 she set aside land for burials from 107 acres she had bought in 1873, signing her name as "X." That land became the Hockley Cemetery.

Though not much is known about this pioneer woman, she must have been a maverick of her era, because she had her own cattle brand YOK and bought her own property despite being Black and a woman. She was married to Wilson Hockley but never took his name.

Becoming a landowner during that era for any woman would have been difficult, said Carey Latimore, associate professor and chairman, department of history at Trinity University. "She's very legally astute," he said. "She's business savvy and knowledgeable enough to ensure that there's something for her children."

In her will, Warren bequeathed her property, including the cemetery, in equal measures to her four sons: Henry Jackson, Aaron Freeman, Alonzo Hockley, and Monroe Hockley. A great-great-granddaughter of Warren still lives on the Southwest Side.

Through the following decades, ownership of the land changed hands several times, Carlson found. Esther Hockley Clay, who died in 1982 at age 101, was the last recorded owner of the cemetery. Turns out the Hockley descendants hadn't staked a claim on the land because they thought they would be charged back taxes they couldn't afford; they weren't aware that cemeteries are exempt from property taxes by state law.

Family members say the last burials took place in 1973. Family lore has it that when the modern-day subdivision was going up at the site in the early 1980s, the driver of a bulldozer clearing the land uncovered human bones and walked off the job, refusing to continue. The story goes that no worker would go back, so the developers simply built around the 1.2 acres. No one knows exactly how many people are buried there.

In contrast to the Hockley and Winters cemeteries, the Griffin Family Cemetery has been maintained as a place of reverence in Oak Ridge Village, near Thousand Oaks and Tavern Oaks, since the subdivision went up in 1990s. Twelve members of the Griffin and Winters families are buried at the grave site. Recently relatives from the two clans met homeowners association president Connie Smith at the gated cemetery that sits near the entrance to the neighborhood.

Smith said the community has embraced the opportunity to honor the former slaves who founded a freeman settlement on the land where Oak Ridge Village now lies.

When Smith moved into the neighborhood eighteen years ago, she was intrigued by the neatly kept cemetery with a granite sign that notes the first burial was in 1900. She did some research and found that the state had issued a resolution for the cemetery. Despite not knowing anything about the people buried there, she and neighbors would gather on the weekends to clean it. "It was the right thing to do," she said.

One time several headstones were vandalized, and a person in the neighborhood anonymously paid to get them fixed. Smith often wondered about the families of those laid to rest at the Griffin Family Cemetery. And then, in a stroke of serendipity, she spotted Fly as he was making his first visit to the cemetery in March. Smith just happened to be walking by with a friend. "It was a God moment," she said.

They started talking and he told her the story. On the day the families gathered at the gated cemetery, Remethia Winters Little knelt and brushed a bit of debris from the face of a stone marker. Nearby Cynthia Young Miller recalled how, as a child, she walked with her family down a road, now Tavern Oaks Street, during funerals to the sprawling oak tree in the cemetery that served as a landmark. The tree towered over the spot where her great-grandfather Horace Griffin's home once stood.

"It's a real discovery," Smith marveled, as she heard the family stories. "It makes it so much more special that the man was a slave. This is a jewel in our neighborhood."

Hindes, the city archaeologist, said Fly's efforts highlight a poorly understood part of San Antonio's past that hasn't been completely explored. "There is so much history, but [still] so much history to rediscover," she said. "And it takes someone who is passionate like

Everett to flush it out. There are valuable stories left to be told and [that] should be told."

For his part, Fly points out that it was Wright's passion and persistence that put the spotlight on the Hockley Cemetery and led to more details being unearthed about the other local Black communities. It's a major find in San Antonio history, he said.

"I give Mike a lot of credit. This makes it clear that Black folks were involved with all kinds of people. They just weren't isolated by themselves. The buying of the land is a major start of civil rights. When you read different versions of the Texas Constitution, it says if a person owned real property they were entitled to vote. It was great—if they owned land they were able to vote."

While the research continues, attention is turning to protecting the site. "We don't want the graves moved, just left alone because of its history," Joyce Harvey, spokeswoman for the Hockley family, said.

That's just what the discoverers are hoping to do. "What we're trying to do is preserve that [land] by letting people know it's there," Wright said. "To me, it's intriguing how everything is interrelated."

Fly said the first step toward preserving Hockley Cemetery is to get a proper and systematic cleaning process started. The ground will have to be cleared by hand, inch by inch, and each fragment of headstone found must be marked. The team is also working with the descendants of the Warren family to establish rights to their ancestors' burial ground.

Clifford Griffin said he and his family appreciate the work that's been done to bring the lost communities to light. "As they died off, the history started disappearing, and the next thing you know, you don't have nothing," Griffin said. "Now that we're getting all of this information back to us, it's great stuff to know we were a big part of San Antonio in the 1800s."

TALES OF SUN AND SHADE

Quiet Time for Dad and Daughter

They sat alone, father and daughter, backs to the world, fishing lines bobbing in the casting pond across the street from Woodlawn Lake. The shaded pool spread below the lane where joggers rounded the lake and children chased geese like wranglers driving a herd. Rodney Castillo and his daughter Bryanna sat under thick cypress trees, their high branches filled with snapped fishing lines swaying like strands from a spider's web. This is fishing time, and it comes when golden daylight and dark shadows float on the water.

Castillo, forty-one, first brought his ten-year-old daughter to the water's edge when she was a baby in a stroller. These days she sits beside him in a vinyl folding chair, casting her line as wide and far as he does. The best thing about their fishing trips is the time with her dad.

Only one thing bothers her. "Smelly bait is the worst thing you can experience while fishing," Bryanna said, sneering. When she needed to bait her line, her father dipped two fingers in a foul-smelling jar, sticking a plug on her hook.

They long for that day when they snag a big catfish, but they don't sweat when, how, or even if it happens. That's the beauty of fishing—they can't control when a fish strikes. They live for the surprise, waiting for the pull of their catch dipping and zipping away with their line. Beyond that, time stops for the pair. There's no talk of topics that bombard the senses, such as war, crime, or money woes. There are just tales of past fishing trips that grow each time they're told. There are stretches of stillness. Small talk melts into silence as they watch their lines drift in the water rippling from turtles skimming the surface and ducks flying in an arrowhead formation.

"We're always forgetting about what God has made for us," Castillo said, reel in hand, leaning forward in his chair. "We need to relax and see things clearly."

This time found others drifting in and around them. On the other bank, a couple sat close on a blanket. Two trees down, five students of the Asian American Task Force–USA recited their divine principle to live as one family under one God. They chose the shores of the pond for a serene site to study their scriptures.

The sun dipped near the horizon, lighting the tree line with gold trim as father and daughter tallied their catches. Bryanna caught two turtles. Both snared minnows, which they tossed back. More than once, their hooks snagged the metal rail their feet rested on.

Castillo's wife comes along sometimes, but often it's just him and his daughter, watching the water. This is their time. It's a time when everything pales in comparison except for baiting a hook and soaking up the scenery—just as it was for Castillo when he was his daughter's age, casting his line by his uncle's side.

Friends in the Park

A young couple delayed their walk down Travis Street, mouths agape, watching a noon feeding in the park. A flock of pigeons encircled a man holding a small white paper plate with a square piece of chocolate cake at the side of a shaded tree. Pedestrians paused on the sidewalk, staring at the man wearing a red baseball cap, denim shirt, blue jeans, and yellow construction boots as he slowly enticed park animals to approach him. As he lowered the plate, two squirrels descended from the branches, spread-eagled and headfirst, like cobras spellbound by a snake charmer.

Biting off a plug of cake, one squirrel skittered into the crook of two branches dangling over the street. The man walked to a bench, watching the squirrels nibble their haul. "He'll sit right there and eat it," he said. "Some people throw stuff at them, but they won't hurt you."

Jeffery Watkins is a regular at Travis Park who whispers to the squirrels and pigeons as he feeds them bits of his lunch and dinner. Many folks in the park are homeless and receive free meals from volunteers serving them at a Mobile Loaves and Fishes truck sponsored by Saint Mark the Evangelist Catholic Church. The four-person crew, one of several, works every first Wednesday of the month, feeding those in need at noon and in the evening.

And many people, like Watkins, forty-four, feed what's left over to the animals at the park. Watkins, a drifter from Pikeville, Kentucky, said squirrels in his town prefer nuts. Squirrels downtown eat everything, he said, including candy, cake, cookies, apples, boiled eggs, bagels, and breadcrumbs.

Watkins knows who's who in the pack. He recognized a small female squirrel, scampering up the tree, by a thin, gray tail. He knows others by the chewed tips of their ears. After tapping the bark, a squirrel snatched a cream-filled chocolate cookie from him, gnawing on the snack held tight between its paws.

Leon Lewis sat on a bench across from Watkins. He pulled pieces from slices of bread and tossed them to pigeons blanketing the sidewalk. Lewis, a New Orleans native, moved to San Antonio nine months ago after Hurricane Katrina. He's ridden the bus every day for the past two months from Fredericksburg Road to the park for meals and to share his bounty. "You get blessings for that," Lewis, forty-eight, said. "They're just like us; they're God's creatures too."

The flock of pigeons rose and fell, breaking apart when a squirrel skittered into their formation and ran away with breadcrumbs. On the other side of the park, a line of more than eighty people who had been waiting for a meal tapered off as the crew shut down their operation.

Bob Taillefer, his wife, Huguette, their granddaughter Jessica Brantley, and Phil Brookes climbed into the truck, ready to replenish their shelves for the evening return. Whenever they have food left over, they drive to the bridge by the SAMM (San Antonio Metropolitan Ministry) shelter and distribute the meals to the homeless. At Travis Park, the crowds spread their leftovers to the animals. Park-goers like Reyes Hernandez Ramirez feed the wildlife bits of their groceries.

Waves of pigeons landed in a gray and black formation as she scattered pinches of blueberry bagels into the air. She spread a handful of crumbs upon the flock like a farmer casting seeds onto the soil. On the fringes of the park, others followed the trio's example, tossing morsels to the small inhabitants, oblivious to life erupting around them.

Four men attacked another man, drawing San Antonio bicycle cops to the scene. A middle-aged man pushed an elderly man in a wheelchair into the shade of the plaza. And Watkins dug into his plastic shopping bag once again for food to feed his friends.

Family Helps Nourish Bodies and Souls under the Bridge

Jonathan Hernandez passes over the Commerce Street Bridge on his way to swim practice every Wednesday morning, crossing over railroad ties and going by rooftop signs advertising bail bonds shops. Unlike many of the travelers, he knows another world exists beneath the concrete lanes. It's a world where he learned that the needs of others outweigh the need to buy the latest cutting-edge electronics. It's a world where people huddle on sidewalks and police in cruisers scan the tide of people moving along South Medina Street. And it's a world where anonymous San Antonio residents offer food and clothing to those without homes, night and day.

The fifteen-year-old Jefferson High School sophomore and his family spend one Saturday every other month ministering to the homeless with their small interdenominational congregation of the Living Word Church at 5800 Culebra Road. Jonathan's father, Jesse, is the pastor. His mother, Irene, sings and serves the street people. His grandparents, Lupe and Margie Cantu, cook sausage, and Jonathan and his cousins set up, serve, and clean up afterward.

For the past three years the two dozen members have partnered with Seeking the Lost Ministries Church, which has called a tar pad under the overpass home since 1997. The Reverend Robert Vallejo is pastor of a church where steel beams serve as the roof, there are no walls, and no one is turned away. "I thank [God] for that roof,"

Vallejo said recently, while pointing overhead and preaching to about 125 members of an ever-changing congregation.

Vallejo turned the microphone over to Jonathan's father, who strode back and forth before a cross-shaped pulpit while delivering the word. "You say, 'Pastor Jesse, you don't know my life,'" he said, pressing a palm to his chest. "But I know the one who does. I know the one who will change your lives if you allow him to."

As Vallejo translated Jesse Hernandez's sermon into Spanish, the crowd raised their arms and bowed their heads. More than a dozen people stepped forward when Hernandez asked who needed a blessing. Some asked for deliverance from alcohol and drugs. Others asked for grace. A weeping man pleaded for a sign of God. As pastors, church members, and the crowd prayed with palms held high, Jonathan and his family prepared to serve dinner. Numbered tickets in hand, the crowd formed a line that curved past tables stacked with donated clothes for a meal of two sausage links, Spanish rice, and beans.

Margie Cantu fished links from a large steaming cooler with metal tongs onto plastic foam plates. They say they never run out of sausage, no matter the numbers. Everyone is fed in a world where shafts of sun slice through shade.

Elf Louise, the Soul of a San Antonio Christmas Tradition

Take flight with the Ghost of Christmas Past and witness the birth of Elf Louise, patron of San Antonio's children. Go back fifty-one years, to the era of moon landings, protests, and the turbulent Vietnam War. The spirit transports you to a Northeast Side home where Trinity University student Louise Locker watches *Tonight Show* host Johnny Carson read Christmas wish lists that tykes have written to Santa Claus.

As Carson reads the letters, a feeling comes over Locker—she could give a girl who never had a doll one from her collection. Locker meets with a local postmaster, asking if she can look through children's letters for a girl likely not to have gifts on Christmas. Impressed by her enthusiasm, he agrees under one condition: he will only open envelopes addressed to the North Pole. Tampering with letters sent to the U.S. Postal Service isn't allowed.

A letter from a girl named Anna changed Locker's life. The girl said her family had never had gifts because she had never written a letter to Santa. She asked for a Christmas tree, a Bible for her mother, and gifts for her and her siblings. Anna ended the letter with "Please don't get lost."

Locker left her meeting with the postmaster with thirteen letters of youngsters who had never had Christmas presents. Her mother, Anne Locker, and several friends joined her to find toys on the children's lists. Two days before Christmas, Locker and a friend stopped at a Christmas tree lot to ask the proprietor to donate a tree for Anna. The grumpy man said, "Which tree do you want to buy?" Locker handed him Anna's letter. As he read the page, tears streamed down his face. "Let me show you our most beautiful tree," he said. He gave them a stunning Scotch pine.

On Christmas Eve a shy friend even slipped on a Santa Claus suit for Locker's cause. They traveled dark streets across San Antonio, squinting to read a crumpled map by flashlight. Serenaded by barking dogs, they delivered gifts until after 2 a.m. The pair delivered the last presents to Anna's home. The girl's mother was stunned by the arrival of Locker and the shy Santa. She had told her children that Saint Nick didn't exist. Anna and her siblings, half-awake, reeled from the sight of the gifts. Locker stood back and watched the wonder unfold. Days later, she was amazed how every door they knocked on in the darkness of night was answered.

They calculated they had delivered close to two hundred gifts to sixty-five children. The visit from the anonymous Santa helpers was the start of the Elf Louise Christmas Project, an all-volunteer organization, which has delivered gifts to 1.5 million children over five decades.

"My hope and dream were that the project would belong to the community," said Locker, now seventy-one. "One of the most beautiful things as the years passed was that everyone would feel ownership of the project. I'm just so thankful [for] all the people who volunteer and the people yet to come."

Five years ago, in 2020, was the first year that Locker wasn't at the helm of the nonprofit. That fall, she stepped down as director, noting that the initiative, made up of five thousand volunteers, is in good hands. Each year, volunteers—San Antonio elves—take new, donated gifts to twenty thousand children up to age eighteen.

At the start, Locker and her team of volunteers worked at her mother's home and her small apartment. As requests and groups of strangers inspired by her cause grew, they moved to donated spaces that included churches, a bank building, and warehouses. For the past seven years, the volunteers have set up at Port San Antonio in a space that resembles a toy shop and Santa's workshop. This year, because of coronavirus pandemic safety concerns, families will pick up the presents and wrap them at home. "It's wonderful that it continues on even during a time like this," Locker said.

She's never been one for accolades and attention. If not for a newspaper reporter who long ago dubbed her "Elf Louise," Locker would still be anonymous. The program's executive director, Bill Harrison, eighty-one, said one of Locker's tenets was that the Santas would represent the community in an anonymous way. Harrison, a retired U.S. Air Force colonel, has volunteered with the nonprofit for thirty-one years.

"We have followed to the letter the project that she set up," he said. "She'll remain the soul of the project forever."

During her time with the iconic operation, Locker, a licensed therapist, has had her own struggles to overcome. A breast cancer survivor, she found hope from supporters and adults who would recognize her and tearfully relate how she had brought them gifts when they were children. "I feel like I'm talking to that younger person," she said. "It's just amazing. To witness so much joy is so touching for me." But she didn't retire because of a medical reason. The Good Samaritan said that with the Elf Louise Christmas Project healthy and strong, this is a good time to step back and explore what nourishes her. She loves being a grandmother, and the opportunity to spend more time with her family was appealing.

This is her time to do simple things such as planting a vegetable garden and learning to navigate the virtual world. She's created meditations set to music for people struggling, and she may delve into writing stories about magic and love. Her retirement gift to herself is a new address book. She plans to be more intentional with the people she loves. "It's nice to slowly connect more with people who matter," she said. "And take more time for that."

There are thoughts of collaborating with others, to help them see and strengthen their dreams, just like her mother encouraged her to do as a child. Locker keeps her mother's legacy alive with the belief that anything is possible if it's wrapped in love. With great patience and perseverance, she said, anyone can make anything happen.

Even in retirement, she's not finished bestowing gifts on the city's children. Locker plans to join the gift-giving campaign with her family in the coming years. But it will be without fanfare, an elf in the night preserving the miracle of Christmas with the goodwill she says lies in every one of us.

FAMILY TIES

Mom's Celebration beyond Mother's Day

Mother's Day has come and gone, but our family never stops celebrating my mother, Valeria Cardona-Trinidad, who lives on in our memories and hearts. Not a day goes by when my three sisters and I don't fondly think about her. Born in May 1938, she was raised by my grandmother Lela Mae Preer Hicks and great-grandparents Willie Lou and Theodore H. Martin. She passed on their life lessons learned in the Heights, a country settlement outside of Phenix City, Alabama.

My mother was a college student during the birth of the civil rights movement, attuned to the changes her generation fought for during a turbulent era. She told stories about her excitement of seeing a young preacher speak at Alabama State University. His name was Martin Luther King Jr.

For the first five years of my life, we lived in Columbus, Georgia, where my great-grandfather, an army master sergeant, had retired from Fort Benning. Mom held the family together as my father, John Davis, an air force sergeant, took us to assignments in South Dakota, Germany, San Antonio, and Omaha. She was easygoing but strict when she needed to be. She raised us with an appreciation for reading and music. Magazines, newspapers, and books graced each room of our house. Volumes of the Encyclopedia Britannica filled a bookcase above a table lined with *Good Housekeeping* and *Jet* magazines and *Stars and Stripes* newspapers. On Saturday mornings we cleaned the house to the sounds of soul spinning from a Grundig stereo turntable.

Marvin Gaye wailed about being chained to love, the Temptations wished it would rain, and the Righteous Brothers crooned that their baby had lost that loving feeling. I can still see Mom humming the Four Tops' "Sugar Pie, Honey Bunch" while dusting. That ritual continued in San Antonio, where my father was stationed at Kelly Air Force Base from 1967 to 1969.

We lived in a one-story ranch house on Reefridge Place near Lackland Air Force Base. On April 4, 1968, I recall my mother calling us inside from roughhousing with friends in the front yard. Martin Luther King Jr. had been assassinated.

While our father served a tour of duty in Vietnam, she found support from other military wives. There were shared dinners and groceries during lean times. Adult conversations took place away from the kids. Worries lessened when she began working as a part-time substitute teacher. Out of those uncertain days, the bond between mothers and children grew stronger. She rose early, making brown bag lunches before seeing us off to Royal Gate Elementary.

Mom stressed that we should study hard so one day we could get a college degree she had to forgo when she started a family. As we moved from San Antonio and became teens in Omaha, she wielded a firm hand. Curfews were in place, and she made sure we knew going to house parties wasn't a right but a privilege. And come Sunday morning, attending services at Salem Baptist Church wasn't a maybe but a must.

Mom was at the start and end of my twenty-two-year air force career. In September 1975, when I boarded a plane back to San Antonio for basic training, she was there. Sitting in my seat waiting for takeoff, I heard a commotion as the flight attendants were about to close the cabin door. It was my mother. She had brought my enlistment package I'd forgotten at home. "You'd forget your head if it wasn't attached," she said, giving me the manila envelope and one more hug.

In June 1997, four days before I retired, my wife, Diane, surprised me by flying my mother to Oklahoma City for the retirement ceremony. She nodded her head at the service when I acknowledged my great-grandfather, a World War II veteran, for his and many others' sacrifices that blazed the way for me and many others.

Through the years, she endured heartbreak and overcame struggles with quiet dignity. She rarely raised her voice at home—a stern look said volumes. Outside the house, she perfected the art of minding her business. It was a calm she fiercely protected, checking the clueless or foolish who tried to test her.

Mom passed in December 2004. My sister Valeria Danielle Middlebrooks called with the news as I finished a Sunday night shift on the cop beat. I held the phone, numb; my eyes filled with tears. The night editor Kerry Cole offered words of comfort, a kindness I'll never forget.

There are family milestones my mother didn't get a chance to see—births of grandchildren she'd never hold and watching little ones grow to have their own families. We missed her presence when I graduated from Texas State University in 2006, the first in my family to get a college degree. Though I wasn't an industrious student, she always believed I could achieve a higher education. She probably would have said, "It's about time."

Her last job was as a teacher's assistant in Columbus, Georgia. It's telling that teachers and aides sought Mom out for her counsel. She shared that same wisdom with us on phone calls, offering calm assurance that, no matter the turmoil of the moment, tomorrow is a new day. We miss her, but family stories and shared memories of our time with her carry us on.

The World According to Madea

A red sun blazed in the sky the day I learned we wouldn't live forever. My four-year-old mind couldn't comprehend what the teenage roughnecks kept repeating: The sun was gonna burn us all up. I burst through our apartment screen door in Columbus, Georgia, screaming until my great-grandmother calmed me down. No, she said, the sun wasn't going to torch the world. Those rascals were just teasing. But, she said, we all were going to die one day. She wiped away my tears and gave me my first talk about life and death. It was my introduction to the world according to Madea.

Willie Lou Martin was our mother dear. We affectionately called her Madea, a southern term of endearment. Her philosophy was simple: There was right or wrong, no in-between. She was our matriarch, born in 1905 when President Theodore Roosevelt began his first full term. She was the second oldest of six girls and one boy, raised with tough love to survive life in a segregated South. Her tenets were formed in a Black settlement outside Phenix City, Alabama. Madea passed her rules down like family heirlooms, forged during the Great Depression, two world wars, and the dawning of the civil rights movement.

Her teachings were brief and blunt. Read your Bible, she'd say, because the good book would keep you on the straight and narrow path. And you didn't want to get her started about approval from others. "So and so doesn't like you?" she'd say with a humph. "That's their business. They don't pay your bills, so why do you care?" Those wise words rang true as I grew older but drew a puzzled look from a kid caught up with cartoons and comics.

Madea's view on race was short and to the point. "We're all the same, baby," she'd say. "Black or white, if we get cut, we all bleed red."

Madea shared her views while indulging in her one vice—dipping snuff. A Styrofoam cup stuffed with tissues absorbed used smokeless tobacco as she watched her soap opera stories. On Sunday mornings, she set the cup aside as she cooked breakfast in her kitchen, rich with the aroma of buttered grits, roasted Maxwell House coffee, and pancakes slathered with molasses. Beside the stove, topped with a can of Crisco shortening, a table radio blared Holy Ghost spirituals and a howling preacher's sermons. Then she'd place one of her stylish church hats upon perfectly coifed hair, a signal it was time to go.

We'd head to Granddaddy's pink Plymouth for the twenty-minute ride from Columbus across the Oglethorpe Bridge to Bethel African Methodist Episcopal Church in Phenix City. Sunday worship was an all-day affair. Madea served as a matron of the church, monitoring manners, etiquette, and those entering the sanctuary. It was before the days of central air conditioning, and hot country air drifted through open windows. Older women cooled themselves and young ones with handheld cardboard fans that bore a halo-lit Jesus on the front and funeral home ads on the back. Political candidates delivered stump speeches at the same pulpit where youngsters, dressed in new clothes and shoes, fidgeted as they recited Easter poems.

During the 1930s Madea helped her family by working as a maid at Fort Benning, cleaning and cooking meals for officers and their families. Her sisters kept her daughter, my grandmother, Lela Mae Preer Hicks, while she worked. Grandmama was our fierce family protector, a story for another time.

My late great-aunt Eula Mae Bellamy recalled the best Christmas gift she received as a child from Madea—a basket of fruit wrapped in red cellophane paper during the Great Depression when many people were going hungry.

Madea met my great-grandfather, Theodore H. Martin, in the late 1930s at Fort Benning, where he served in the army. Married in 1941, they raised my mother, Valeria Cardona-Trinidad, with values that saw them through trying days. Madea was proud of my great-grandfather's military service. Like scores of spouses, she kept their household going while he served in World War II and the Korean War.

When Granddaddy retired, they settled in Columbus. After years of living in an apartment, he used his GI Bill to buy a one-story, red-brick home in the suburbs. Madea kept a pristine house, a refuge where glass candy bowls heaped with sweets encircled *Jet* magazines on the living room table. The pantry was always stocked with groceries from the post commissary. Madea was always ready to make our favorite meals. Her only caveat: finish what we asked her to cook, a byproduct of living through the Great Depression.

In the late 1970s I'd travel from Lackland Air Force Base for an annual visit. Her only request was that I wear my air force dress uniform at church. I wore it when I saw her in August 1982 before leaving for a three-and-a-half-year assignment at San Vito Air Station, Italy. "Go on, boy," she said after a hug and nudge to the door. I returned in summer 1984 with my wife, Diane, and our eleven-month-old daughter, Brittaney. It was the last time I saw her. Several months later, her heart gave out. I returned alone for her funeral.

Madea's final resting place is along the two-lane country road where she was born. Wild stalks of amber corn sprout from the red soil of the cemetery, which dates back to after the Civil War. My great-grandfather never returned to her grave. It dredged up too many memories.

Madea's legacy lives on. In an age of brands and a social media tell-all landscape, her sayings may seem obsolete, but not to our family. Her teachings still resonate, ringing with simplicity and truth.

Granddaddy Passed on the Magical Art of Spinning Tales

Theodore H. Martin had a thick mustache and hair combed back with Old 97 hair grease. Smoking Hav-A-Tampa cigars, he spun stories that transported listeners to war-torn lands, dark country roads, and fire-lit cabins. Listeners left doubled over from laughter and dabbing away tears. I can still see my great-grandfather sitting in his den in Columbus, Georgia, regaling fellow World War II army veterans and relatives with outrageous tales that defied belief. Adult family members called him Sarge. Fellow army veterans called him Mr. Martin. My great-grandmother called him Pietro. To my sisters and me, he was simply Granddaddy. But he had another name: storyteller.

It was from Granddaddy that I learned the magical sway of stories. My youngest sister, Jeanine Fields, recalled hearing his scary tales drifting from the living room when older folks visited. It was the first time she heard the word "haint," often used down south for "ghost." "Every detail was enlightening and enriching," she said. "It seemed so real, like you were there."

As a youngster I would sit on an old three-legged stool, listening to Atlanta Braves broadcasts on Granddaddy's transistor radio late at night as he barbecued slabs of ribs for picnics at Bethel Baptist Church in Phenix City, Alabama. Other kids and I would sit on the church steps, teetering paper plates piled with food on our knees.

Everyone chewed on grilled meat slathered with his secret sauce that made us drip with sweat. We sipped from cold soda cans that had been submerged under crushed ice in the bed of a pickup parked on red dirt.

Granddaddy only gave his stories a rest on Sunday, which was reserved for hours of worship in the red brick church off a black two-lane gravel road. Relatives said he became a churchgoing man after returning from the death and carnage of World War II and the Korean War. He'd rise early, wearing a handkerchief tied at the four corners that pressed down his salt and pepper waves. Then he would slip a tailored jacket over a pressed shirt and stylish tie. The cuff of his creased pants brushed the top of black shoes buffed to a shine. The finishing touch was a sharp, dust-free fedora.

My mother, great-grandmother, sisters, and I would climb into his Pepto-Bismol pink Bel Air with rear twin fins pointed like tips of arrows. I'd stare at the endless dark green water of the Chattahoochee River flowing beneath the Oglethorpe Bridge as he drove us from Columbus to a day-long service in Alabama.

In 1962 I was six when we left with my father, John Davis, an air force sergeant, for assignments that took us to South Dakota, Germany, San Antonio, and Omaha. During our travels my mother, Valeria Cardona-Trinidad, kept Granddaddy's stories alive with friends at gatherings.

Close family friends Ruth Mitchell, eighty-four, and retired air force chief master sergeant Thomas J. Echols, eighty-eight, recalled egging her on to tell Granddaddy's stories decades ago in Darmstadt, Germany. It was a time when airmen and their families met at Echols's base housing, where our mothers cooked collard greens, ground beef, and big pans of cornbread. The kids played board games away from the adults, who played pinochle and told stories of growing up in the South. "It's the way we survived two or three days before payday," Echols said. "We learned to entertain ourselves."

Mom's standout story was about the town drunk harassed by the police. The stories still have meaning today. Mitchell said the Black community's relationship with law enforcement hasn't changed. "Every time Val started telling a story, I remember it," Mitchell said. "We've come a long way, Vince, but we're not there yet. But we have someone to take care of us. And when He gets tired He'll fix it for us."

After I enlisted in the air force in 1975, I'd visit Granddaddy, my great-grandmother Willie Lou Martin, and grandmother Lela Mae Preer Hicks once a year. In letters, we wrote "mother dear" when referring to my great-grandmother. In person, we called her Madea (long before Tyler Perry's character of the same name arrived in the mainstream). Married for more than fifty years, she'd heard all of Granddaddy's tales. Shaking her head, she'd say, "Martin, stop lying." Her reproach spurred him on even more. In 1984 he placed his stories on hold when Madea passed.

Years later we'd sit in his backyard, sipping from bottles of Heineken as he rehashed family lore. He'd tell stories of serving in the segregated army, where he was a drill sergeant at Camp Croft, South Carolina, training soldiers to survive in hand-to-hand combat. During World War II, his company, staged in England, was confined to the camp. The higher-ups didn't want Black soldiers fraternizing with the English. Granddaddy and other sergeants convinced the officers to allow the soldiers off base, on a limited basis, before they departed to fight in Belgium.

When he retired from civil service, he focused on turning the yard into a massive vegetable garden. Wearing a sweat-stained, straw cowboy hat, he tilled the soil and grew rows of tomatoes, cucumbers, and greens, just as he had growing up in Georgia.

Spinning tales was the most he ever talked. In public, a man of few words, he rarely talked about politics and never about other people's business. He'd watch the evening news and grimace as scenes of civil rights protests, war, and poverty played on the television screen. The one thing he did, a must for him, was exercise his right to vote.

Granddaddy told stories until 1995 when incurable diseases brought our family to his side for his last days. Sitting in the front room, we could hear visitors howling as he told a rib-tickling tale with a raspy delivery. Then there was silence. That was his last story. Four days later he took his last breath.

Still, we've carried on his tradition, telling his stories to our children and grandchildren like adding new patches to an old quilt. His tales live on with each retelling. And so does he.

CHEF'S TABLE

Tea Cake Lady of San Antonio

People say Gloria Bryant's tea cakes are like warm sunshine that melts in your mouth. There are stories of grown women weeping with joy after tasting her version of the old-fashioned dessert. Others say the tea cakes take them back in time to their grandmothers' kitchens. And it's not unusual for those who see her carrying the southern delicacy to swoop upon her and lessen her load.

Bryant's pastries are well known at Second Baptist Church on East Commerce Street, where she brings the treats for special occasions and for families who have lost loved ones. There, she's called the Tea Cake Lady, a title she's had since refining a recipe passed down from her mother. She's one of the last bakers keeping alive a culinary tradition practiced by cultures around the world.

The recipe for tea cakes is thought to have arrived in America in the 1700s when the English settled in the Deep South. It later became a fixture in African American households. Bryant's friend Ella Saine says many young people aren't familiar with tea cakes, but once they taste the vanilla- and nutmeg-flavored dessert they become disciples.

"It's made with a lot of love; you can't throw that together," Saine says. "I tried [to make them], but they came out like rocks. You might have the recipe, but it won't turn out right if you don't have that touch."

Elbert Mackey of Austin, author of *The Tea Cake Roundup*, says finding an original tea cake is hard these days, and that prompted him to request recipes from bakers via the Internet. He received more than two hundred responses.

A woman from Georgia says she used a Royal Crown Cola bottle as a rolling pin. Some people used fork tines as their personal stamp. Mackey's aunt, Maggie Wimberley, used her thumbprint.

His family would drive north Louisiana dirt roads, spewing clouds of dust behind the car, to Wimberley's house, where her handmade sweets were always ready for guests. At age nine, Mackey took up the old southern ways of cooking and baking.

"It's something about not having a mixer," he says by phone. "Everything was done by hand; three hundred strokes to stir the batter."

Mackey says enslaved people took a bland treat and incorporated West African methods to give it flavor. In the post-slavery years, they'd slip a taste to their children, who grew up and passed the recipe to their descendants.

"All the ingredients were readily available—sugar, flour, buttermilk, eggs, and flavoring," he says. "It was a dab of this and that; they kept it in their memory."

The delicacy peaked in the mid-twentieth century, when it was the dessert of choice among African Americans on Sunday afternoons after church.

Each time Bryant whips up tea cake batter, she says it stirs memories of her mother, Cleona Price. As a child growing up in Beaumont, she wasn't that fond of the tea cakes her mother made on weekends. There were always batches around for Bryant and her ten siblings.

The recipe came from her great-grandmother in Louisiana, who spoke more Cajun than English. When Bryant was fifteen her grandmother died, taking her recipe for homemade ice cream with her.

"It's why I wanted to learn the recipe," she says. "I've tried to pass it to the next generation."

She's currently teaching her niece, Lydia, and daughter, Jan, how to bake the dessert. Bryant's lessons began thirty years ago.

When women at the church started bringing dishes to functions, she decided she would bake tea cakes. But first she had to learn how to make them, so she drove four hours to Beaumont to watch her mother bake the golden pastries. When her green 1970 Cadillac sedan rolled into the driveway, her mother greeted her at the door, ready to give another lesson.

The first few times her efforts came up short. It took several trips to Beaumont for advice from her mother. Her husband, Dr. Frank Bryant Jr., the first medical director of the Ella Austin Health Clinic, supported her as she strived to duplicate her mother's success.

"I just didn't give up," Bryant says. "I kept at it until I got it right."

Her mother died in 1997. Now Bryant is the keeper of the family's sweet heirloom.

Four years ago Helen Embry was one of a dozen women from Second Baptist who visited Bryant for a baking demonstration. The women learned the process step by step. They learned everything must be precisely done. And they learned nothing starts until the butter has softened.

They watched as Bryant slid a pan of dough into the oven, then stood back and watched through the window for three minutes as the cakes began to rise. When the glaze disappeared, Bryant turned the switch to broil until the tea cakes browned—one more batch that kept an old custom alive.

"She's just a wonderful person, loved by all," Embry says. "Tea cakes have been a wonderful ministry; people adore her for that."

The Martin Luther King Jr. Service Guild at Second Baptist honored Bryant with a certificate that recognizes her contribution to a cultural experience. "It said, 'Tea cakes take you back home,'" Bryant says. "People enjoy the taste that takes you back to your roots."

Honey's Place a Throwback to 1950s Nightclubs and Soul Food Stops

Far out in Bexar County, between Martinez and China Grove, is a spot called Honey's Place, where no one is a stranger and good times are in large supply. Owned by La Rita "Honey" Brown, it's a throwback to old-school nightclubs, such as the legendary Eastwood Country Club, where integrated crowds gathered in the 1950s and 1960s on Saint Hedwig Road some twelve miles away.

A popular place for special events, birthday bashes, and the occasional wedding, Honey's sells food, beer, wine, and soda; if a customer's choice is liquor, they can bring their own.

"It's a lot more modern than the old juke joints," Brown, forty-nine, said. "The feel is still the same."

The disc jockey plays what the patrons call "grown folks" music from the soothing rhythms of India Arie to the sweat-stained blues of Marvin Sease. Men in cowboy hats, fedoras, and baseball caps sidle up to well-coiffed women dressed in outfits that sparkle and shine.

In the pre-COVID-19 era, pulsing lights glowed in the dimly lit space and lively conversation muffled the crack of spinning billiard balls. Regulars sat at an outside spot called the Bee Hive, smoking cigars, drinking, and laughing. On Saturdays the corrugated steel and wood building was packed to capacity and servers had to turn people away. On Sundays the club converted to a restaurant serving soul food Brown cooked in her food truck, called Honey's Kitchen.

Because of the pandemic, the club now operates more as a diner. Tables are set up outside where customers are masked and practice social distancing—as best they can—through the night.

Located at 7119 Joe Louis Drive, it's tucked into an area still defined by customs of the African Americans who settled there more than a hundred years ago. They owned farms and raised horses, and descendants still know roping and other stockman skills. For decades generations of youngsters rode donkeys, horses, and cattle on land owned by a man locals called "Mr. Chicken."

Long gone are other ice houses and night spots that marked a social ease in which older folks would sit outside and wave to passersby. Rusted tractors rest beyond pastures maintained with twenty-first-century riding mowers. Brown's relatives lived out here, and memories of the laid-back, friendly atmosphere led her to open the club two years ago. "I opened for the history and to support Black businesses, and upgrade the standard of what people expected," she said.

The road, named for the famous Black heavyweight boxer of the 1930s and 1940s, is "literally where the whole culture of San Antonio changes from city to country," she said. The location was once a mechanic's shop, and it took Brown more than a year to convert it and to clear five acres with help from friends and family. She installed air conditioning and heating, brought in furniture, and installed rustic columns from timber cut on the property.

She sells eleven-dollar dinners on Soul Food Sundays, arriving early to prepare dishes such as smothered pork chops, stewed turkey wings, neck bones, fried fish, and chicken. Accompanying sides include macaroni and cheese, candied yams, dressing, greens, cabbage, Cajun rice, and corn.

"She does a good service for the community," said Earlie Satterwhite, seventy-three, a frequent visitor. "It all comes together."

A 1989 John Jay High graduate, Brown grew up on the West Side with her mother, Frances Perryman Brown. Her father, Wilmer Brown, taught her to cook, a skill that enabled her, as a single mother, to generate extra income to help her two older children pay college tuition. In 1993 she became enchanted by the nickname of a woman who took her under her wing when her mother died. Brown recalled the woman telling her, "You would be a good 'Honey,'" a term of endearment from her grandchildren.

Brown started selling food plates and saved $2,500 to buy her first food truck eight years ago. She moved up to small events and a bigger truck three years later. It was a financial gamble, and she decided buying land was more of a sure thing. Her vision is to move from weekend ventures and take her business full-time.

She'll have plenty of help. Among several family members and neighbors who back her at the club is Robert Shaw, who owns Lightning's Arena across the road. And there's Allen Eugene Banks, who runs Allen's Golden Corral, which offers horseback riding and lessons.

Before Brown arrives from her day job, the pair start readying things for the evening. Banks, sixty, works the door on club nights, collecting tickets and making sure folks are dressed correctly and everyone has a mask (if not, there's no entry). "She's like my little sister," he said of Brown. "I love her to death."

Brown plans to continue the area's tradition of celebrating forebears by honoring her late mother, who died of lupus. She plans to start a nonprofit called Frances's Legacy Lives, which will host a two-day fundraiser, "A Taste of the Country," featuring a trail ride, dancing, and Black-owned vendor booths. Brown said a portion of the proceeds would go toward the Lupus Foundation.

As durable as the country way of life has been, change is on the way. The area is flourishing with new neighborhoods and large companies alike. Brown is preparing for the day when the city fully arrives.

"I want to make sure I'm a staple," she said, "and provide a feel of the old times."

Chef Gives Ten-Year-Old Direction

Wisps of steam rose from a pan on the stove where ten-year-old Victoria Taylor sautéed marinated pork chops with strips of green pepper, onion, and sliced mushrooms at her North Side apartment. In a white chef's jacket, her hair tied back with a pink bow, the young chef drizzled brown gravy on white rice and baked asparagus spears at 400 degrees in olive oil. She seasoned her entree and sides with selected herbs and spices, but Victoria's favorite flavoring is Slap Ya Mama, a Cajun seasoning she uses for "all that goodness."

The fourth grader washed used pots and pans as she cooked. Everything—the spatula, ladle, and glass dishes for the food—had a place on the counter. She completed each task with discipline, order, and focus, ingredients once missing from her life. The young chef caught her dinner guests off guard when she greeted them with the phrase, "Today I have prepared for you," as if on the set of the Food Network show *Chopped*.

Her mother, Tori Warford Scott, no longer has to worry about preparing dinner for her family after long days at work. Cooking has been Victoria's joy, but that wasn't always the case. Until a year ago the youngster, diagnosed with attention deficit hyperactivity disorder, needed redirection for disruptive behavior when the family lived in Houston.

She wasn't passing her classes, and her conduct at school was always unsatisfactory. Scott, a single mother, juggled working as a geriatric nurse, tending to her family, and responding to emails and calls from Victoria's teachers. The nurse found support from family and friends. Her mother offered prayers. Her two older children helped care for their little sister. She enrolled Victoria in sports such as soccer and volleyball, but the youngster wasn't interested. Scott worried about the rising cost of medication, some that left her daughter lethargic. "It was day to day trying to get Victoria through a day," she said.

Then Scott mentioned her dilemma to Chef Milas Williams, a family friend who knew firsthand about second chances. "Let me work with her," he told Scott. "She's going to be okay."

Williams, a former gang member, ran the East Side streets in the 1990s, and by age nineteen was sentenced to twenty-five years in prison for aggravated robbery. Culinary classes were his key to a new life and release from prison after fifteen years.

Scott said enrolling Victoria in Arrow Academy, a charter school that emphasized discipline, and Williams's tutelage were the turning points for her daughter. Williams introduced the youngster to another level of cooking. Though 197 miles away in San Antonio, Williams answered Victoria's questions and gave her pointers online via FaceTime and Google Duo video apps.

The man Victoria calls "Mr. Eli" taught her discipline. He taught her that everything in the kitchen had a place and purpose. He taught her how to keep a clean workspace, prepare different cuts of meat, and respect the skills of an honored profession. Williams, forty, said he was honored to be in Victoria's life at a young age and help get her off to a better start. "People who already have a career need to make themselves available if they give their word to a child," he said. "The reasons some children grow up with a dysfunction is because of voided promises. Then we wonder why some kids turn out the way they are. People need to stand on their word."

Last year Victoria and her family moved to San Antonio, and

Williams continued tutoring the youngster at his workplace, Grill on a Hill. In October she worked by Williams's side at his Thanksgiving outreach event, one of the programs of his nonprofit World LOLEI. It gave her a glimpse of how food could lift the spirits of those who have little or nothing to eat during the holidays.

"When [Williams] entered her life, it was a 360-degree turnaround," Scott said. "She found her desire in life was to be a chef. That's what she wants to do."

Scott said Victoria is no longer on ADHD medication. She's able to focus, even if she needs redirection. Scott has received reports from Victoria's San Antonio teachers that the troubled child in school records from Houston wasn't the same child in their classes. When Victoria received an E on her report card, she asked her mother what it stood for. "Victoria, that means that your behavior is excellent," her mother replied.

That behavior has expanded beyond the kitchen. She writes recipes from YouTube cooking videos in a journal. She has her own set of knives that no one else can use. She also wears an apron her grandmother bought with her name embroidered upon it. Victoria is currently studying to take her food handler's exam.

In the future she wants to compete in the Food Channel's Junior Chef competition and open a restaurant called Victoria's Cafe. Until then, she hones her skills cooking dinners for her mother and sisters—Cyani, thirteen, and Kortni Warford, twenty-five. Victoria's siblings said the strides their little sister has made changed her life.

"I'm really proud of her," Kortni said. "Seeing her come from where she was to where she is, is just awesome. That's my pride and joy."

Victoria's family, including grandparents, were present July 17 when she was honored at Williams's sixth annual Community Junior Chef Competition at the Kitchen Campus, 3014 Rivas. She prepared a dish of shrimp and grits with her mentor. Afterward Williams called the youngster to the front as several chefs gathered around her. They handed a starched white garment from one to another as induction into their ranks. Williams presented Victoria with the white jacket representing discipline, responsibility, and respect.

She beamed as family and guests applauded her ascension to the culinary world, a galaxy away from the days of disorder and disruption. She proudly held up her jacket, embroidered with the words "Junior Sous Chef," a title that says she's ready for more responsibilities not only in the kitchen but also in life.

Chef Wants Teens to Avoid Mean Streets

Weeks ago, ten families received phone calls that they were nominated anonymously to receive a Christmas shopping spree. Many recipients were skeptical, but it wasn't a scam. On Saturday morning Milas Williams welcomed the families to the Unity in December event at the Walmart store on Austin Highway.

His nonprofit World LOLEI sponsored the event and allotted each family $1,000 to buy gifts and necessities. Between aisles 13 and 15, Williams and his team prayed with the grateful mothers, fathers, and children. They received free T-shirts from chef Johnny Hernandez and his family, supporters of the nonprofit's cause. The excited children and their happy parents then headed out to the store aisles, filling their shopping baskets with clothes, toys, and household goods. "It's not every day something like this happens," Makeisha Wallace, twenty-nine, said as she chose clothes for her three children.

The eyebrows of Jacqueline Cardena, twenty, and her mother, Maria, rose above what surely were smiles behind protective masks as each woman pushed a cart clanging with cleaning products and toiletries. "To see the looks on their faces was monumental," Williams, forty, said through a camouflage mask. "This is the true meaning of Christmas. What better way to celebrate Jesus Christ's birthday than to give back."

In 2014 Williams, his brother Detrick, and Athena Williams founded World LOLEI, which stands for "Loyalty over Liberty Equals Integrity." The Christmas shopping spree was the organization's newest event. For the past five years Williams has hosted the Youth Empowerment Thanksgiving Dinner and the Junior Chef Competition. The nonprofit also sponsors three families bimonthly, paying utilities, expenses, and rent to relieve burdens brought on by the pandemic.

An executive sous chef at Oak Hills Tavern on Fredericksburg Road, Williams and his organization aid families in urban communities and offer opportunities to San Antonio youths.

His road to becoming a humanitarian was paved with trial and error. Williams grew up in the East Terrace neighborhood, among the New Light Village apartments, one of several gang turfs on the East Side in the late 1980s.

Bullet casings littered the sidewalks. Sneakers swung by shoelaces from power lines, a sign in this neighborhood that someone had been killed. Drug dealers and prostitutes populated the streets but suspended their activities when children walked by. His mother, Marshell Williams; stepfather, Tracy Allen Stevens; and father, Curtis Duhon, raised him, three sisters, and two brothers with love, morals, and values, yet Williams was drawn to the temptations of his environment.

He was eleven when he joined the East Terrace gang and took on the lifestyle lived by some of his uncles and cousins. Williams said he wasn't as notorious as some of his street peers, but he did his fair share of mayhem. He was nineteen when his crimes caught up with him. He was arrested for aggravated robbery and sentenced to twenty-five years in the state penitentiary.

One year in the Texas criminal justice system brought salvation and saving grace, he said. Mentors from all walks of life and a culinary program internship helped Williams evolve. After five years he was eligible to enroll in a careers program. Cooking was one of his favorite things to do with his mother and grandmother, so he chose a culinary program. That led to the San Antonio Food Bank Second Chance culinary program.

"Our life is like a recipe," Williams said. "The different ingredients in our lives are like the different people in our lives. We're all defined by the ingredients of our success."

His list of benefactors is long and diverse. There were Dana King, a female detention sergeant at a unit near Houston who believed in him when no one else did, and Bobby Stanton, an older inmate who shared sayings by Confucius, bits of wisdom that Williams still quotes. He learned about respect from Joe Thompson, a weightlifting trainer serving a life sentence.

Monday through Friday, he would wake at 6 a.m., line up, and walk to culinary class. From 6:30 a.m. to 1 p.m. he worked on skills that would open doors to a promising future. There were recipes that didn't turn out right, and his instructor had Williams cook them up again. And again.

A member of a prison gang taught him how to make biscuits and cornbread at a prison kitchen in Abilene. He also taught the future chef an important lesson. Williams was puzzled by the intricate techniques the white cook used to bake a cake.

"Hey, how did you learn to cook like that in prison?" he said.

The man pointed to his head, and said, "I never got locked up here." Then he pointed to the skin on his arm and said, "I got locked up here. As long as I'm free in my mind, I'm still a baker like I was in the world."

Williams was released early after serving fifteen years. He graduated from Saint Philip's College culinary school and credits his success to chefs that include Hernandez, David Gates, JoJo Doyle, Ruben Luna, Brian West, and David Delgado. He said his nonprofit's contributions wouldn't be possible without his family, donors, and team members. Williams said his staff, directors, and supporters know youth served by the nonprofit by name and stay in their lives to offer an alternative to the gang life. Their work is in the name of East Side icons such as the late Reverend Claude Black and former councilman Joe Webb.

"They were like our Moses," Williams said. "And our Martin Luther Kings and Malcom X's. They were superheroes in our community. I want these children to keep their innocence. Every child wants to feel like they are a superstar at an event. We know these children."

His mother has always known her children had promise. She's cried for the boy who cooked by her side, grew into a teen prowling with gangs, and was jailed as a young man for his crime. Now she cries tears of joy whenever she sees her evolved son on television sharing his story.

She cries, Williams said, because her prayers for his deliverance from evil have been answered.

Taco Church Ritual Carries On

Their place of worship doesn't have a steeple. Sunlight doesn't filter through stained glass windows, because there aren't any. There's no dress code. And you won't find pews. What you'll find each Sunday morning are like-minded souls at the unlikeliest of chapels—El Milagrito Cafe, an unprepossessing breakfast and lunch place that for decades has anchored one end of the North Saint Mary's Street nightclub strip.

Congregants call it the "Taco Church" and have made it a weekly ritual to gather there over steaming cups of coffee and chilaquiles norteños to talk family, work, and politics. Waitresses hand out menus as a mere formality—they already know the group's menu choices. The slap of high fives and loud laughter blend with the chatter of diners and Tejano tunes spilling from speakers. The racket is in lieu of solemn alleluias—but before dining, the church members do perform one sacred rite. They bow heads and tent hands to say grace and amen. They sometimes refer to themselves as "the Village." They're artists, business owners, corporate executives, health care administrators, law enforcement officers, political consultants, scholars, and teachers.

Taco Church stretches back to 1975, when community activist and the group's organizer, Andy Hernandez, first met Willie Velasquez, who was founding the Southwest Voter Registration Education

Project. Hernandez, now seventy-one, was the first person Velasquez hired. They talked strategy over tacos. "It's always had a special place in my heart," Hernandez said of the café. "It reminds me of that time and it's great food."

Each Sunday as many as fifteen members might arrive around 9:30 a.m., before parishioners from nearby churches crowd the restaurant. Our Lady of Sorrows is less than a block away, Trinity Baptist is walking distance, and its event facility, TriPoint, is even closer. San Antonio has a tradition of movers and shakers doing much of their political work out of restaurants, breaking bread in fellowship to discuss events and support one another. In decades past, former civic leaders and politicos of the Snake Pit Society met at Mi Tierra restaurant in Market Square, and some still do.

During the late 1960s into the mid-1970s, young Chicano movement activists met at Mario's Restaurant on the near West Side. Founding members of the Milagrito crowd originally met at a River Walk pub and called themselves Los Juevesitas (which can be loosely translated as the Thursday Bunch).

Hernandez, who became the Southwest Voter Project president after Velasquez passed, is the congregation's linchpin. He has mentored, taught, and worked with members who include Delia Garcia, the first Latina and youngest state representative of Kansas, and Patricia Mejia, vice president of inclusive engagement with Spurs Sports & Entertainment. Teresa Niño, the vice president for external affairs at the University of Texas at San Antonio, said the most important part of Taco Church is "purpose." "That's what Taco Church does for us. It's generational and good living."

Garcia said their lives are intertwined through births, marriages, career achievements, divorces, and funerals. "This is like my chosen familia. Here is where I always felt welcomed, loved, and not judged."

I first met the group at the café working with photojournalist Robin Jerstad on a column about eating my first breakfast taco.

Political consultant Laura Barberena invited me to their table to partake in the weekly ritual. She said El Milagrito is their venue for two reasons: exceptional food and the multiple generations of influential figures who have gathered there.

"It's an opportunity to talk about the news of the day," said Barberena, who has a doctorate in communication studies. "We talk about leadership, politics, social and economic issues." Hernandez's ties run deep with Barberena; he was the officiating pastor at her marriage. Members said her husband, Anthony Medrano, is a leading voice on the significance of mariachi music in American experience.

Raised Catholic, he coined the name of the group and its ritual. "Taco Church" came to him five years ago while he was having breakfast at a Mexican restaurant where there was a live broadcast of a San Fernando Cathedral mass on TV. The thought of merging tortillas and a television church service was a revelation.

"I get to eat tacos and go to church," said Medrano, director of Mariachi USA at the Hollywood Bowl. "It's a joyous celebration of being."

Last Sunday photojournalist Arthur H. Trickett-Wile and I returned to the café to hear the group's banter, which rolled across two tables and a booth beneath a string of festive-colored *papel picado.* There was wide agreement on most topics—except for an ongoing friendly debate over the merits of tacos versus avocado toast. Nora Herrera and Mejia, both avocado advocates, said the dish was a healthy breakfast alternative. Medrano disagreed. "If it's wrapped in a tortilla, you can't go wrong," he said. "My grandmother never woke me up and said, 'You want avocado toast, mijo?' I'm just listening to my ancestors' voice." A guest supported the healthy choice.

Actor Tony Plana, who has starred in more than two hundred films and television shows, including *Ugly Betty*, *JFK*, and *The Good Fight*, stopped by the service before he was honored at the San Antonio Film Festival with the Texas Yanaguana Award. Plana founded Seniors in Play, which offers older San Antonio residents ways to express creativity, improve self-esteem, and empower themselves through the arts. He said being with the Village filled his soul. "It's a beautiful idea. People get a chance to really interact. In some ways, it's a lighter version of confession."

Mejia brings her seven-year-old daughter, Karolina, to experience what it means to be part of a community. Karolina, she said, is the future. At home the youngster talks about girl power and getting her first presidential election T-shirt, a reflection of the passage of time at the communal catch-ups.

"It's walking through life together in times, good and bad," Mejia said. "It's incredible as a mom to witness. She's walking away knowing she has a responsibility to show up differently. And it happens here."

Mejia sees Karolina absorbing concepts as she colors pictures. And in the heat of a policy discussion, a member will ask the young disciple how her day is going and color with her. "It's just like people, but about food," Karolina said of the church, toying with crayons. "It's love."

A Whole Breakfast in a Taco

Breakfast tacos are the meal I never knew I needed, until it was thousands of miles out of reach. In the early 1960s you couldn't find breakfast tacos, or tacos of any kind, on menus in Columbus, Georgia. As kids, we awoke to the clamor of our great-grandmother stirring, mixing, and frying our morning meal. The aroma of bacon, eggs, toast, pancakes, waffles, and grits (with butter and salt, not sugar) wafted from the kitchen into every room of the two-story apartment.

It wasn't until after 1975, when I enlisted in the air force, that I discovered the Tex-Mex standard. I tasted my first breakfast taco in 1978, while stationed at the 3700th Supply Squadron at Lackland Air Force Base. Thanksgiving was days away when Anita, our supervisor, called us together at 7:30 a.m., before the workday began.

With a pen and flip notepad in hand, she asked each person their preference. When she asked me, I shrugged my shoulders. I didn't have a clue what a breakfast taco was, let alone what choices were available. After telling my fellow airmen to stop laughing, she explained what the meal was and its menu options. "Carne guisada," she said. "I think you'll like carne guisada."

She was right. The mix of beef stew and brown gravy remains my top choice; second is the no-frills refried beans with cheese and bacon. Anita taught novices like me breakfast taco etiquette.

There was a thoughtful manner to the taco order experience—she favored certain spots on the West Side, but for expediency often opted for a taqueria outside of the base's Valley Hi gate. Before meal runners left to get an order, she'd remind them to bring back plenty of red salsa, sealed in small plastic tubs. While we waited, anticipation was high. The runner arrived carrying brown paper bags, the bottoms damp with grease.

A lull fell over the room as Anita pulled out each foil-wrapped tortilla packed with various fillings. She read our choices written in black marker on the outside of the thin, crinkled wrappers. When there weren't markings, she unwrapped each taco to find our orders. It was a ritual for the ages.

Ordering breakfast tacos was the priority of the morning. On delivery days, before we loaded supplies onto blue pickups, we consumed many tacos and washed them down with hot black coffee or cold soda. It was a good day when a sergeant said the magic words, "I'll buy, you fly." Forgive my fuzzy memory about the price of a taco in the late 1970s, but it probably cost less than a dollar, which we were eager to keep.

Over the years I've learned more about the breakfast taco. I've gained a better understanding of its origins and how it's a heated topic between Texas cities touting which one serves the best tacos. All I know is, like many transplants from other states, it's become a staple of morning fare.

While stationed at bases overseas and across the country, those of us who have lived in San Antonio would commiserate about missing the South Texas breakfast item. As all military members do, we dealt with our dilemma by adapting to our surroundings and the local cuisine. At Ramstein Air Base, Germany, several of us craved sausage, eggs, and cheese in a warm flour tortilla. Many mornings my wife lamented not having a scrambled egg and bacon taco from a small kiosk on Marbach Road.

Servings of Wiener schnitzel, jägerschnitzel, rahmschnitzel, and cordon bleu helped ease the pain. At San Vito dei Normanni Air Station, Italy, three and a half years of antipasto, pizza bread, and pasta with marinara sauce made things a bit better. Our landlords, Ma and Pa Cavallo, helped by sharing dinners in their home, where they served vino; soda was forbidden.

At our favorite restaurant, the waiter would bring my preferred dish: spicy penne all'arrabbiata along with Tabasco sauce to pour on more heat, if needed. In the mid-1990s the Alamo City breakfast taco was eight hours away by car when we were stationed at Tinker AFB, Oklahoma.

By 1997 San Antonio was our home, and we promptly resumed eating breakfast tacos. In 2003, on Saturday mornings at the *San Antonio Express-News*, weekend cops reporter Elaine Aradillas brought tacos to the newsroom from her go-to spot: El Milagrito Cafe near Trinity University.

Sometimes I'd make the taco run to the café, where I learned the art of adding toppings to the breakfast staple by listening to other customers' orders. Pico de gallo. Grilled onions. Jalapeños. Limes. Guacamole. Cilantro. Peppers. Sometimes I asked the cashier for a combo that made the tortilla bulge like a water-filled balloon about to burst. "Dang, partner," the cashier said one morning. "You don't want a taco, you want a burrito."

Amador Montoya said the breakfast taco is one of the biggest sellers at the restaurant his father, who has the same name, and mother, Juana Palacios, have owned for the past twenty years. The Sonora family owned El Milagrito from 1969 to 2004, when Montoya's family bought it. "Every day, we see the same customers from the seventies and eighties," said Montoya, forty-one. "It's changed a bit because of the pandemic and gentrification. They're still coming back, even if they've moved to Bandera and Boerne."

He said that on a busy morning, they'll serve more than two hundred to-go breakfast taco orders to customers who include city workers, parents dropping children at school, military personnel, and college students. Originally from Monterrey, he said that after two days back in the Mexican state of Nuevo León, he hungers for a tortilla and the fixings. "That's a San Antonio thing. It's a whole breakfast in a taco. They don't do that there."

I've made up for years away from the mecca of morning meals. No more worries about missing the breakfast staple. It's only a taqueria away.

Line Up for Ruben's Tamales

A San Antonio tradition began sixty-five years ago when a hungry man stepped into an East Side drugstore, opened in 1952, curious about the savory aroma that drifted from a back kitchen. "What's that I smell?" he asked Helen Perez.

"I'm cooking dinner for my family," she said. "It's tamales."

"What are those?" the Anglo man said.

She gave him a tamal on a plate. He was hooked. He came back the following week. "If you make any more of those, I'll buy some," he said.

The man's craving for the Mexican dish offered Ruben and Helen Perez a new business plan—selling tamales. Business had been bleak since a new Handy-Andy opened nearby, but the family's fortunes changed for the better when they reopened as Ruben's Homemade Tamales. For many San Antonio residents, lining up for tamales at the family-owned store is an honored Christmas ritual.

This is the Perez family's seventy-second anniversary serving people from all walks of life in and beyond San Antonio. Two living children of five, along with nieces, nephews, and relatives, keep the operation going. Rosa Linda Perez manages the store; her sister Sylvia Pickrell and her husband, Karl, handle the financial accounts.

"We're the only ones left," Pickrell said. "We ended up saying, 'Let's run the store together,' so that's what we did."

Rosa Linda Perez said their family includes all twenty-five employees, especially the women who work hard and make tamales the old-fashioned way. The whole family worked in the kitchen, where they returned after going to school, getting degrees, and working. "These are our machines here—our hands," said Perez, who started in the kitchen when she was six. "We're traditional."

The only filling sold in December is regular pork for $13.50 plus tax. Throughout the year they offer bean, chicken, and jalapeño pork. Without a measuring cup or spoon, the ladies spread chili powder, salt, and lard into the dough. They thrust their hands into the mixture, churning and turning it until they achieve a peanut butter consistency. They spread the masa through stacks of corn husks next to red plastic vats topped with pork.

Pickrell said they cook three thousand pounds of lean meat each night. The wrapped tamales go in water-filled steel pots that steam on the stove in the next room. Isabel Chavez, a forty-one-year employee, completed each step with ease. She said December is a special time when they see people with happy faces in the store. "We have the same recipe, workers and same hands," Chavez said. "That's why the flavor is the same as it was fifty years ago."

Friday was the last day of one-hour waits for the sought-after tamales. From now until Christmas, wait times will run up to four hours. In the past customers have arrived as early as 3 a.m. for a place in line at the store, located at 1807 Rigsby Avenue. As they edge their way to the door, they scroll through texts, chat on cellphones, and make small talk among themselves. The wait inside starts between a beverage-filled freezer case and a wire rack stuffed with chicharrónes, chips, and Cheetos. People inch forward beneath papier-mâché piñatas and fiesta banners dangling from white ceiling tiles. Shelves stocked with cans of Wolf chili are the halfway point.

When customers reach the counter, thirty-five-year employee Marvin Lee often rings up the sales. He bids each client goodbye with a receipt and parting message of "God bless you, and Merry Christmas."

The sisters' brother, Francisco "Frankie" Perez, brought Lee, his best friend, into the fold. Lee, a navy veteran, said the parents looked out for him. He recalled how Helen Perez said that as long as they owned the business, he had a place of employment. "I'm not at work," he said. "This is my home. I'm bound by honor to look out for them."

Ruben's has been Raul Hernandez's go-to spot for the past ten years. Friday morning he bought twenty dozen tamales for a Christmas party at his home in Austin. He said the ninety-minute drive, overnight stay, and early morning visit are all worth it. "I feel like they taste the most homemade," Hernandez, thirty-seven, said. "You just know it's going to be a perfect tamale."

Pickrell said customers also drive from places like Houston, Dallas, and Floresville. They stop by as early as mid-September to stock up on the dish that draws families together on Christmas. Some patrons ship bags across the country and overseas. Pickrell said she'd heard someone mailed homemade tamales to the Vatican.

Teresa Clay-Sattiewhite, fifty-six, bought six and a half dozen tamales for her daughter Jasmine Tumblin in Bremerton, Washington. The wrapped masa, warm in aluminum foil, wouldn't be in San Antonio for long. Three hours later it was in her carry-on luggage on a flight to the Great Northwest. "I'm willing to share with my neighbors in the row," she said.

Around noon Luis Rodriguez, twenty-nine, from Alamo Molino, delivered the second load of masa that day. He said he drops up to a thousand pounds of masa at the store each day. "They sell a lot. They don't play around!"

Much has changed since a hungry stranger fell in love with the Perez family dinner decades ago. But not the aroma that still wafts through the space. And not the customers, from far and wide, who still file into long lines beneath the sign that bears the family's name.

LIFE'S TINY SURPRISES

Tiny Surprises Add Joy in Hard Times

If the friendly mother of three had her way, no one would know she's the mystery person leaving surprises in her North Side neighborhood. No one would know she's the one leaving colorfully painted stones beneath bramble and brush. No one would know she's the one who twist-ties jokes, printed on paper and sealed in clear plastic, to the chain-link fence surrounding Northwood Elementary School. Only her family and a few neighbors would know that it's Lisbeth Anne Dunlap who's the secret spreader of good cheer. Until now.

Her husband, John Dunlap, fifty-five, persuaded her to share her story of uplifting her neighbors to take their minds away from pandemic troubles. "I didn't want to draw attention to myself," Lisbeth Dunlap, fifty, said. "This has gotten me through the coronavirus."

She's among countless people who have responded to the pandemic with kind acts toward others. There have been reports of car parades for birthday celebrants, food donations for out-of-work restaurant employees, people applauding health care workers from balconies. Her husband said his wife isn't someone who can stand by and do nothing. "In her way, she needs to be a part of the healing. It's her therapy. She loves it."

Now residents will know she's the same person who puts a table of puzzles in her front yard for passersby to put together or take home. She is also the same person who lined the roots of a tall live oak tree at the edge of her front yard with illustrated rocks. It's not unusual to see wide-eyed toddlers scramble on the spot she named the Northwoods Rock Garden filled with stones scattered around the tree.

Grown-ups and children have added their own painted rocks to the collection. "It makes it their garden, which is really cool," Dunlap said. "That's the best part about it."

Recently Joshua Cooper, thirty-eight, stopped at the curb with his two young daughters. They gazed at the stones featuring images of a Smurf, peacock, snail, and shark. There's a brick painted with the words "Have Courage, Be Kind." And it's not just in the Dunlap yard. The painted rocks are scattered throughout the neighborhood.

Cooper is one of many residents out for morning walks who were taken by the painted random rocks in other gardens and near the curbs where Dunlap left them when nobody was looking. "I think it's really lifted people's spirits during a time when they're looking for things to feel good about," he said. "It's been a bright spot during the last few months. It's something that adds a little variety. You never know what you'll see or find."

Dunlap's humanitarian deeds are familiar to her children: Calvin, twenty-four; Jonah, sixteen; and Emmy, seven. Also familiar to the siblings is their mother's enthusiasm for life. Breast cancer made her realize that she had to live a life of service to others. That epiphany led to missionary trips to Burundi. In 2014, on her third visit to the East-Central African country, she met eleven-month-old Emmy. That led to the couple adopting their daughter two years later. The young girl who loves glitter often walks with her mother to put up the jokes. They have a special makeup day when they apply lipstick and mascara to each other's faces.

Dunlap's acts of sunshine are carefully planned. On Sunday she prints out her jokes and takes down the old ones. The next day she replaces new jokes in the plastic sleeves. Here's an example: "What do you call a rock that never goes to school? A skipping stone."

Wednesday brings Puzzle Day, when Dunlap puts out a puzzle

exchange table, with a bottle of disinfectant, on her front driveway. Just as fast as people take them, new ones arrive. Thursday is Painted Rock Day, when she places the stones she's painted throughout the neighborhood; some are in easy-to-find locations, others take a bit of work to find. Those who live in the area have shared how the random gifts have reaffirmed their hope in humanity.

Dunlap's goodwill has been lauded on Nextdoor; some have taken pen and paper to show their appreciation. Recently she received a card from an anonymous resident who had lost her job and was feeling hopeless in this time of sweeping change. "Please know that you are a gift of life," the neighbor wrote. The card ended with, "The tiny pieces of art you have shared along my lonely path have given me a reason to be alive."

Another neighbor addressed Dunlap as "Dear Rock Gardener," thanking her for "lifting our spirits during the virus days!"

Dunlap's acts aren't for praise or acknowledgment. She'd be fine remaining behind the scenes, unnamed, creating small pieces of art. Knowing she's added a small spark to her neighbors' lives is the gift that keeps her going.

Friends Share Bond through Window in the Fence

Most mornings, in these days of isolation and social distancing, Laurel Forney runs with light footfalls across a path of flagstone and pebble to her shaded backyard fence. Once there, the five-year-old lifts a square hatch built into the wooden fence at her eye level.

"Miss Dian?" she calls, peeking through the peephole. "Hello, are you there?"

On the other side of the fence Dian Coppin, seventy-four, spies the open portal. Beneath a strand of clear light bulbs and tendrils of ivy, she sits to talk to her little friend. The pair talk animatedly about all kinds of things, such as tinkling wind chimes and the sweet taste of cherry tomatoes that Laurel's parents grow in the yard.

"She adds to anybody's day," Coppin said. "I call her the giving girl."

Their relationship began a year and a half ago, when Coppin found a child's plastic arrow in the backyard of her Northwest Side home. Hearing chatter on the other side, she asked if anyone had lost a toy. Laurel, then four, said yes. She clambered up on a tree branch and peeked over the six-foot-tall fence. It was the first of many meetings.

Laurel has also surprised her friend with treasures, leaving them tied to a red push pin at the base of the window. A hawk's feather. A painted glass circle that resembles a mermaid's scale. A kaleidoscope of butterfly stickers and a seashell. Coppin in turn dangles gifts over the fence for Laurel and her three-year-old brother, Fox, who stands on a turned-over old pot to peer through the opening.

At first Laurel would climb from tree to tree to see Coppin, followed by Fox, who tries to do everything she does. On her side of the fence, Coppin stood on a bench to talk to her small friends. Abbey and Travis Forney worried that their children might slip and hurt themselves.

They asked Coppin and her husband, Anthony, if they could make an alteration to the privacy fence. The Coppins were fine with their neighbors' proposal to build a little window into the fence so Laurel would have a safer way to talk to her neighbor. As soon as they said yes, Travis Forney, thirty-seven, took just fifteen minutes to get the job done using a jigsaw. He cut out a piece of fence slat, added a hinge to it so it could be opened upward, and installed a hook so it could be latched open.

Travis Forney said the window, located beneath green leafy branches, reminds him of a scene that would fit right in the children's show *Mr. Rogers' Neighborhood.*

"It's my peephole," Laurel said.

The youngster's conversations with Coppin are always interesting. Last week she listed the names of dragons from the animated movie *How to Train Your Dragon*, as a hawk's shrill call echoed in the distance. Sometimes they talk about toads that dwell around a gurgling water fountain that rests beside the opening. Coppin, who has grandchildren of her own, listens intently to Laurel, who has become familiar with her neighbor's family.

On Mother's Day Laurel opened the window and introduced herself to Coppin's relatives, who were there for a social distance gathering.

"We didn't see Dian in person very often," Abbey Forney, thirty-eight, said. "It's really neat to get to know your backdoor neighbor. She has a special friend during a time when she doesn't see many people who are not her family."

Coppin and her family moved to their home six years ago from an area where there were few neighbors around. The friendship she has with her young neighbor has restored her belief in community and the value of shared experiences.

Abbey Forney knows that in the future, memories of the pandemic and the changes it wrought may linger with her daughter. She hopes it won't be just reflections of masks, isolation, and keeping a six-foot distance from one another. Forney hopes her daughter will always fondly remember Miss Dian and their wondrous portal into each other's world.

Downtown Mystery Siren Solved

For eighteen years a mystery has plagued Maria Z. Aguillon. A loud siren can be heard across her downtown office every workday at noon and 5 p.m. It reminds her of the work whistle that blew on the 1960s animated show *The Flintstones* when it was quitting time at the Slate Rock and Gravel Co. But where is it coming from?

Aguillon, payroll manager at Goodwill Industries of San Antonio on West Commerce Street, across from Market Square, and her coworkers came up with a range of theories about the source of the whistle. They eliminated the old Bexar County Jail; it was torn down in October, and the shrill blasts continued. Aguillon thought maybe the whining whistle she heard from her second-floor office came from a factory across downtown. Coworkers said they'd heard it as far away as the Bexar County Courthouse and the King William neighborhood. Last week Aguillon set out to research the source of the siren that has perplexed her for years. Her answer came from the unlikeliest of places: an office down the hall.

She mentioned the mysterious whistle recently to creative and digital manager Lauren Serrato, thirty-nine, who casually said, "Oh yeah, that's the Bill Miller whistle."

Aguillon, fifty-five, was crestfallen. She couldn't believe the source was Bill Miller Bar-B-Q headquarters, just two blocks away on Santa Rosa. "I'm so disappointed. I just needed to know about this mystery. I never thought it was from Bill Miller."

The revelations from coworkers kept coming. Trina Hibbard, senior marketing and workforce administrator, said she learned two years ago that the sound came from the brick building. Hibbard, sixty-three, first heard the blast a few years ago above her as she entered the building for lunch. Janet Ward, director of marketing, said she discovered the source six years ago. "It's been a staple for all of us," said Ward, forty-nine. "It's our clock, too."

Roxanne Mijares, social media manager for Bill Miller, said the siren is an air horn the business bought from a train company in the mid-2000s. A valve opens, and the horn bellows for thirteen seconds from the roof of the commissary-bakery twice a day. "Balous Miller—son of original owners Bill Miller and his wife, Ila Faye Miller—wanted us to get a workingman whistle to let everyone know about lunch and time to go home," Mijares said.

During daylight saving time workers adjust the settings of the horn that has contributed to many San Antonians' downtown work experience.

Aguillon's joy in discovering the source of her curiosity may be short-lived. The company, which operates more than seventy restaurants in and around San Antonio, is rumored to be moving its headquarters to the West Side, to a site at the northwest corner of Texas 151 and Old Highway 90.

The coworkers said they would miss hearing the whistle that became part of their workday. Serrato jokingly said she's going to tape the siren for nostalgia's sake. "I can record it in its full glory."

SPREADING CHEER

Ex-Gang Members Spread Cheer Not Fear

With a rap on the door, Christmas came early for Rebecca Carrillo and her two babies. Her gifts came courtesy of former West Side gang members who turned their lives around and came together to give back to families in need in the old neighborhood where they were raised, called Ghost Town. Leonardo "Lalo" Mendez, sixty-six; Luz "Louie" H. Gallegos, sixty-six; Juan Guajardo, sixty-five; Hector "Pro" Caldera, sixty-five; and Alfred "Curly" Palacio, fifty-nine, are members of a group called the Ghost Town Survivors. Their stop at Carrillo's home at the Alazán-Apache Courts was the first of three visits the men made to deliver gift baskets laden with goodies.

After delivering the Carrillos' gifts, the men said a prayer for the babies and single mother, who doesn't have a job but is getting her GED and trying to get ahead. Carrillo's basket overflowed with toys, large bars of chocolate, brie, a turkey, and other holiday staples and $355 in gift cards. She was shocked. "Wow, I'm overwhelmed so much, by how this Christmas they'll be able to get more things than last year," she said.

The men were drafted during the Vietnam War and served their country far from friends who spent years in prison or died violent early deaths. Through the military, they traveled and learned there was a world beyond their gang territory and gained a new perspective on life. Many earned college degrees and found good jobs.

Others fought for Chicano rights and helped veterans in need. Now fathers, grandfathers, and great-grandfathers, the men formed a club of sorts with eighteen members to help families who come from the same streets they did. They envision a future where they help seniors once a week and offer scholarships to neighborhood teens. Caldera said the group members hope their acts will ignite similar generosity among former gang members in other parts of the city.

"Hopefully, other barrios will find out what we're doing and give back," he said. "Each one of us made it out because a person made a difference in our lives. That's what this is all about—giving back."

"That's what we're about, giving back to the neighborhood we grew up in and were able to get out of," Guajardo said.

From 1962 to 1968 the men roamed turf that ran north and south from Saltillo to Guadalupe Streets and from Hamilton and Barkley Streets—an area where young men were automatically in the gang just by virtue of living there. Some said the area may have gained its "Ghost Town" name for being a sparsely populated wooded area at one time, scattered with small houses.

The first wave of youth gangs burst on the scene in the 1950s. According to a federal probation report, by the end of that decade gang warfare accounted for up to six fatalities a month in San Antonio. Mainly confined to the South and West Sides, the gangs had colorful names like the Austin Street Gang, Alazán-Apache, El Circle, Los Palo Altos, and La Tripa. The men remembered newspaper reports that called their territory "notorious," but they didn't see it that way at the time.

"Everybody thought it was normal back then," Guajardo said. "We didn't think it was a dangerous place to be; it was our home."

The neighborhood was full of young tattooed men hanging out on porches, men who taught the boys to watch their backs at all times and to always remember anyone they fought with—in case of retaliation. "I aspired to be like that," Mendez said.

Many of those young men of the barrio met violent deaths at a young age. The gang members often scrapped in front of Saint Timothy Catholic Church, where many of the men were baptized, made their first communion, and said their wedding vows. They said it was an area where police officers only drove through in the daytime and arguments were settled by stabbings or shootings. They fought with their fists, bats, bottles, and whatever they could get their hands on. Many have multiple stories of being shot at leaving a dance or walking down the street.

Several members have physical reminders of their younger-day rumbles. Guajardo still bears the scars from when a rival slashed his face. When he was fifteen he was involved in a gang fight at La Villita and was packed into a police wagon with twenty-nine other gang members and taken to jail. He still remembers his mother scolding him because she had to take off from work to go with him to juvenile court. There was their fifteen-year-old friend who was killed after he was stabbed thirty-seven times. Caldera recalled another friend of the group, a guitar player who had his own band and a baby on the way, who was killed. A gang member from another turf shot him in the back in a drive-by in front of the Good Samaritan Center.

After the funeral Caldera grabbed a knife, jumped into his 1954 Chevy, and went to look for the shooter. People recognized that he was driving a car from Ghost Town, slamming their doors and running, as he drove through the projects, hoping someone would attack him. No one did.

"To us, that's the way the world was," said Mendez, a retiree of thirty-two years in civil service. "We were lucky we made it."

"We survived for a reason," Guajardo said. "God had his hand on us. He said, 'You're going to go through life, you're going to have your downs, and when I think you're ready, you're going to come out of that.'"

In between delivering gifts, the men visited old homes where they grew up. Mendez, one of thirteen children raised by his grandmother, showed the group his apartment at the Cassiano Homes.

He used to shine shoes, sneaking through a hole in a wire fence at Lackland Air Force Base to polish airmen's boots. Decades later he worked a couple of blocks away from those barracks as a budget analyst.

"The military drafting me was a blessing," he said. "It exposed me to a new society. The military allowed me a skill. I'm very grateful I'm not one of the victims of the neighborhood."

After graduation Gallegos was sent to Vietnam. Mendez, the last son in his family, was sent to Germany, exempt from the war under the sole survivor rule. The army drafted Guajardo after he graduated in 1968. He fought in Vietnam and was wounded in the Mekong Delta when he stepped on a land mine. He was awarded the Purple Heart and spent months in rehabilitation at Fort Sam Houston.

After leaving the army he took up another uniform with the Brown Berets, a grassroots civil rights group that fought against police brutality in his old neighborhood. Caldera is retired from the Veterans Administration, where he helped veterans from all wars with post-traumatic stress disorder and now works as a social worker. He served two tours in Vietnam and said the veterans talk about how seeing blood and bodies in the barrio helped them become numb to the violence of war zones.

"I made a U-turn in my life," said Gallegos, who turned his life over to God ten years ago. "I'm not proud of some of the things I did."

The nucleus of the Ghost Town Survivors was formed by Mendez, who began calling old friends to socialize and reminisce about the good old days. Each month they met at different West Side restaurants and noticed while driving past old streets that not much had changed since they moved away. They still saw families living in poor conditions and kids running the streets. They wanted to tackle the poverty in the area and decided to give out gift cards with hope the recipients would buy food and clothes for themselves and their children.

They partnered with the Good Samaritan Center, a place they considered a second home and a haven from gang warfare. They held a barbecue fundraiser in early December to add to the donations collected from members at each meeting. At the benefit, Father Michael DeGerolami from Saint Timothy Catholic Church blessed the group's project after picking up two plates.

"I like to think of it as a tree of life," Gallegos said. "We're the branches that are bearing fruit."

The group sold more than two hundred tickets and raised $2,300. After buying toys and gifts with the money raised, they gave each of three families three gift cards totaling $355. The men took a break from gift-giving on Thursday to eat lunch at one of their old hangouts, Ray's Drive Inn on Nineteenth Street. Oldies played from speakers as they talked about reconvening after the holidays to start extending help beyond gift-giving. They plan to help feed families and seniors at the Good Samaritan Center once a week, talk to school kids about getting out of gangs, and offer two scholarships to neighborhood students.

Late that afternoon they drove to the final home. Raymond Gonzalez, his two daughters, and a son were surprised when the men stepped through the door bearing big bags stuffed with gifts. Mendez bent down to hand Gonzalez's son a GI Joe. "We had to look very hard for this," he said, referring to driving to several stores across town before finding the toy.

Gonzalez thanked the men as his wide-eyed kids emptied their bags.

"That's what we wanted, for their eyes to light up," Mendez said. "This is why we want to insert ourselves into their lives, even if it is for a couple of days."

Santa Claus of Fredericksburg Road

The Santa Claus of Fredericksburg Road rumbles down cracked sidewalks in an electric-powered wheelchair, his black belt dangling in the wind. Clad in the traditional red and white uniform, he greets all with a wave limited by cerebral palsy. His fake beard hugs the contour of his chin, trailing like a running dog's tongue. But it itches his head, so he stuffs it in the back pocket of his wheelchair. A whistle hangs around his neck for times when he has to stop traffic to pull away errant grocery carts or acknowledge the pretty ladies.

Santa Claus is just one of many roles that Carl Bringer, forty-nine, plays during the festive times of the year. On Halloween he dresses as a clown with a rainbow wig. During Fiesta it's a giant sombrero. And between holidays he sports a Texas-sized cowboy hat or an angler's hat with fish pins. "I just do it for the holidays," he said, after returning from a recent afternoon trip. "I don't like to be cooped in."

He's a familiar sight as he rides more than two miles on the round-trip route from his home at the Fredericksburg Place apartments, down Vance Jackson Road, beneath an Interstate 10 overpass, to the Walmart, and back. But Bringer's mode of transportation is just one of several differences between him and the jolly bearded one. Bringer gets by on his Social Security check, with Medicaid for his medicine. His North Pole is a Section 8 apartment he's lived in for the past ten years. Elves didn't sew his suit; he bought it off the rack at a flea market on Bandera Road.

His friend Olga Frias said Bringer has gone through a lot. A few years ago someone stole his Santa suit, she said. There have been times over the years that neighborhood toughs, looking for money, have jumped him. And Frias is afraid he'll be run over one day while spreading his holiday cheer. "He hides everything," Frias said, pushing a walker across the parking lot to the nearby Goodwill Super Store. "He doesn't show that he has a problem in the world. He enjoys life."

But none of these things have pushed him off course. Recently a small boy, holding his mother's hand, slowed to look at the mobile Santa as he rested before leaving the parking lot of his apartment complex. Bus drivers and motorists honked their horns as he sped onto his route past the shade of the Goodwill store, gunning his electric chair to the middle of the four-lane road.

Tons of steel roared by as Bringer waited for a gap in the flow of traffic. Then he zipped out, pushing a toggle stick with one hand and waving to passersby with the other. During the week, he returns home around 2 p.m. to watch *Let's Make a Deal* and power his chair.

His holiday run is put on hold as he plugs a cord from a red socket below his seat into a wall outlet. When the charge light on his chair turns green, he's back on his way. Many people wave back. Some pedestrians take a double look, giving a wary wave, as he passes them. Others have greetings of their own. "Tell him to keep out of the street!" a man yelled recently from a passing car at his apartment complex. "He's been hit four times this year already!"

Bringer said the last time he was struck was after Thanksgiving in a hit-and-run accident. He said the impact totaled his wheelchair and threw him a few feet onto the street. He rides in a wheelchair that's on loan, still making his jaunts across traffic.

Annette Anderson, manager of his apartment complex, has watched Bringer roll along the busy street for several years, with his shifts of persona depending on the season. "I think he has a lot of spirit," she said. "Though he's handicapped, he has a lot of life. He's a very unique gentleman."

The Santa Claus of Fredericksburg Road rolls along, passing out all of the tidings and joy that he can afford—a fading wave and a lingering memory.

Community Lifts Spirits of Former Santa Claus

For years Carl Bringer dressed as Saint Nick, navigating his electric wheelchair along asphalt and cracked sidewalks, waving to passing motorists as the Santa Claus of Fredericksburg Road. He wore the old-school Santa suit: black shin coverings, red coat, pants, and hat, all ringed with white faux fur. And there was an itchy, fake silver beard he often stuffed in the pocket of his wheelchair. Having cerebral palsy limited him, but it never stopped his rides along the busy street lined with risks.

Then, in 2017, he was struck by a car, the fourth accident in several years. His close friends Kathy and David Walden helped Bringer move to Brookdale Senior Living to get needed care.

Recently he told another friend, Paul Stahl, that he was sad; he missed waving to folks along the busy midtown road. Stahl's wife, Bexar County district court judge Catherine Torres-Stahl, had an idea. She posted a request on Facebook for folks to send Christmas cards to Bringer and lift his spirits, as he had done for so many people.

Cards started arriving last week. Some were postmarked from beyond San Antonio, as far away as England. Bringer was shocked by the outpouring of goodwill. He was as excited as a youngster opening presents on Christmas morning. "I was surprised," he said. "The cards came all at the same time. I need to find a way to thank them."

On Tuesday afternoon twenty-five friends gathered at Mamacita's Mexican Restaurant at Interstate 10 West to celebrate Bringer's sixty-first birthday and let him know they're always thinking of him. The Waldens arranged Bringer's bash, his first birthday party in ten years. Applause broke out when he arrived wearing a birthday cake hat with "Carl" embroidered on the bill. Friends gathered around him for hugs and photos. They set up a corner table to hold a cluster of balloons and a basket filled with a dozen of his Christmas cards. There was a birthday cake with a photo from a 2010 *San Antonio Express-News* story about his holiday cheer.

Cliff Cavin, an artist and evangelist, blessed the ceremony, those assembled, and his cousin Carl. A few well-wishers shared how they met their friend. Stahl met Bringer more than twenty years ago as he steered his wheelchair through the Deco District.

Stahl, fifty-four, said his friend had never met a stranger. "He's got a gift. As isolated as he feels, he still has this gift to reach out and connect. I hope Carl knows how many people love and think about him."

Volunteer coordinator Patricia Gonzalez, thirty-seven, shared how last June she and hospice volunteer Charles Fisk helped get a motorized wheelchair from a family whose loved one had used it before he died. It wasn't long before Bringer was road-testing the chair at a high rate of speed. "I had to tell him to slow down," Gonzalez said.

Bringer calls the wheelchair his Ferrari. Friends also shared details of Bringer's past. They said he grew up with siblings near Castroville during hard times. However, they didn't mention why Bringer has always spread tidings of joy. That's his personality, the way he's always been.

"It was a gift God gave him," said David Walden, seventy-seven.

When he met his wife, Kathy, she made it known that Carl was part of the package. In 1986 she learned about Bringer's generosity when he called her landline phone. He was in the hospital with a broken neck from his first car accident. He was dialing random numbers to wish people happy Thanksgiving. Friends said he still makes the calls.

When the phone rang thirty-five years ago, she picked up and talked to Bringer, unlike others who hung up. Walden said it was fate. A year later she randomly met him along his route two blocks from her home. She was walking with her two daughters on Bandera Road and Skyview when she saw a young man fall to the ground. When she asked his name, he said Carl. She learned he was the same man who had called her.

Walden, seventy-three, moved to Dallas for six years, and when she returned to San Antonio she saw Bringer along Fredericksburg Road. "By the third time, I got the drift," she said. "It was a God thing. Anything we can do for him, we'll do it. He's like a son."

Over the years the Waldens have helped their friend stay self-sufficient, navigate Medicaid issues, and set up medical power of attorney. They remembered how Bringer was a welcome sight along Fredericksburg Road.

Though known for his years of Yuletide greetings along the busy street, Bringer is a man for all seasons. He wore a clown outfit and rainbow wig for Halloween. For Fiesta he donned a huge sombrero. On Easter he dressed in an Easter bunny outfit. No matter his ensemble, motorists and bus drivers honked their horns as he stopped and darted through traffic on the four-lane road.

Bringer faced more challenges than traffic when he left his federally subsidized, Section 8 apartment at the Fredericksburg Place complex. Someone stole his Santa suit once, and four men stole his motorized wheelchair. There were times when area toughs accosted him for money and broke into his apartment. Now he finds comfort in his room listening to music on his Amazon Echo smart speaker and looking over mementos from years past. One of his favorite songs is Bill Withers's "Lean on Me." He treasures an autographed photo of his idol, actor John Schneider from the *Dukes of Hazzard* television show.

On December 6 David Walden accompanied Bringer as he waved at passing motorists. Bringer was stationary, but it was fine.

Some things never change. The beeping and honking responses from drivers were back in Bringer's life. He was outside in his element again. And the smile, spread across Bringer's face, was the same as it was back when he was the Santa Claus of Fredericksburg Road.

BONDS OF THE GAMES

Willie Doria's Glory Days

His bat of choice was a Louisville Slugger. Year after year Willie Doria played baseball in the unforgiving Texas heat, sweating in a thick wool uniform without complaint. His superpower was sharp eyesight that enabled him to zero in on a pitcher's grip and slam whatever ball was thrown his way.

In San Antonio baseball circles, Doria is highly respected as a pioneer of the game. He's renowned for hitting homers at ballfields across South Texas as a player on numerous teams from the 1940s to the 1970s. Today, at ninety-five, the lively Doria is still in the game, albeit from a different perspective. He supervises the players' entrance for the San Antonio Missions and is an interpreter for Spanish-speaking baseball players who come from Latin American countries. He's in his twenty-sixth year with the Missions and shows no signs of slowing down. Recently he sat down with lifelong friend Joe Sanchez, seventy-four, in Sanchez's trophy room, reminiscing about decades of glory.

Sanchez is the last president of the Spanish American Baseball League, which was to Latino players what the Negro Baseball League was to African American players in Central and South Texas. Surrounded by gleaming trophies and old jerseys lining the walls, they recalled Doria's batting prowess.

Sanchez said it's a shame his friend's caliber of talent wasn't nationally recognized. "Mr. Doria is a legacy in himself. Back then, local Hispanic ball players were all given the same opportunities, so to speak, but knowing they were never going to reach that major league level because they were not allowed to go that high."

In 2015 Sanchez spoke at the University of Texas at San Antonio's Institute of Texan Cultures presentation "*Los Peloteros*: Baseball in the Tejano Community" about the cultural impact of early baseball players in Texas barrios. "These *peloteros* paved the way for every Tejano child who's picked up a bat and dreamed about the big leagues," said Greg Garrett, a museum researcher at the institute and coauthor of *Mexican American Baseball in the Alamo Region*.

Doria was one of those children. He was eight when he first stepped onto the crumbled gravel surface of Lambert Street on the South Side. Barefoot and brimming with energy, he gripped his bat—a broomstick handle—and waited for the pitcher's fastball. When the homemade ball, nothing more than a cluster of string and twine, spun his way, Doria recalled smacking it high into the sky, sending it out of sight. It would be the first of countless balls he would hit beyond a fielder's reach.

Service to his country suspended his pursuit of his favorite pastime. A year after World War II broke out he enlisted in the navy, lured by the recruiter's siren song of Hawaii and hula girls. The eighteen-year-old never made it to the islands, however, instead serving in the Pacific on the USS *Saratoga*. After the war he returned to San Antonio and married, had three children, and resumed batting balls over fences in the Spanish American League, playing on Fred's Team and Grand Prize Beer teams, among others. A rare ticket to the pros came in the form of an invitation letter from the Boston Braves to try out for third base on March 3 at spring training in Temple in Central Texas.

Doria clearly remembers the date because his younger brother committed suicide the day before that scheduled audition. Family members said he should keep the appointment despite the tragedy, but it didn't seem right to Doria. His fifteen-year-old sibling had always sat in the grandstands and supported him as he played, and the emotional ties were too strong for Doria to leave home then. "He was the first death in the family," he said, his voice cracking. "I couldn't do it."

In 1957 he enlisted in the air force for what turned out to be a twenty-year career working with secret aircraft surveillance that he still can't talk about. But he continued playing baseball in the military, hitting home runs for teams at various bases that he hesitates to identify. He takes his oath to Uncle Sam seriously.

Sanchez's friendship with Doria goes back to the day Sanchez was born. They both chuckled that for some unknown reason, Doria was at Sanchez's house when his mother gave birth. In the 1950s Sanchez's father, Sandy Sanchez, relied on the slugger's skills and always penciled him in as the closer on the team roster. Sanchez told stories of how his friend hit home runs that were on par with two pros of that era. At Pittman-Sullivan Park, he smashed a ball four hundred feet over the same fence that New York Yankee Mickey Mantle had cleared during an exhibition game and the same one San Antonian John "Mule" Miles had homered with the Negro Baseball League.

Sanchez said Doria's best home run came in 1989—at the age of sixty-five—when he put the San Antonio hitmaker in a pickup game and he blasted a bomb out of the park, well over the heads of the awestruck younger players. Sanchez said that, sadly, there aren't any ledgers left that recorded Doria's batting average or other statistics he earned during his baseball career. But Doria doesn't dwell on real or imagined slights. His grip is still as strong as it was decades ago. As is his memory of the satisfying crack of a bat on Sunday games at fields that no longer exist, such as the Polo Field at Brackenridge Park and Sanchez Spencer Field.

"On these fields, a man was not defined by the color of his skin or what side of town he was from," Garrett wrote in his book. "He was defined by his ability to throw a ball, swing a bat, and field with a glove."

That's the way Doria remembers it.

Rodeo Riders Go for Fun and Glory

Kickers Korner rodeo arena in southwestern Bexar County is a place where old wranglers spin tales of the days when they rode eighteen hundred pounds of lightning out of a chute. They always emphasize the past tense. On Sunday they matched injuries in a friendly game of one-upmanship—a broken back here, a cracked collarbone there. Sitting on the top of an old wooden table, they watched a new generation prepare for their shot at joining the exclusive bull riders club and possibly riding a bull for the mystical eight seconds.

The young men draped a gray metal fence with ropes and equipment. They peeled off clothes and pulled on riding gear. They strapped on chaps, spurs, and protective vests and slipped in mouth guards. They taped wrists they hoped could withstand the force of the bucking Brahman bulls on the other side of the fence.

Every Sunday family members, friends, and rodeo fans fill the bleachers to watch what has become a ritual in these parts near the town of Atascosa. Most riders sixteen and older pay ten dollars to compete in the Jackpot Rodeo, which veterans said has been around since the birth of rodeo. Younger riders don't pay; they just practice. But everybody signs a release that doesn't hold owner Jim Mathis liable for injuries suffered during the event. Admission to watch the twenty to sixty contestants ride bulls and hold on for glory is free.

Mathis, sixty-nine, has owned the land since 1973. He said the arena was used in the film *8 Seconds*, the biography of bull rider Lane Frost, starring Luke Perry.

"Some are looking for thrills," said Billy Blessing, fifty, who leases the land from Mathis for the event. "Some are looking to be world champions one day."

Blessing, a former rodeo clown, said 99 percent of the area riders who rode in the Professional Rodeo Cowboys Association, the PRCA, started at the arena. That's a tradition twelve-year-old Troy Garcia plans to continue on this particular Sunday. He has been in training since he was four, riding sheep, calves, and now miniature bulls.

The riders today come from all walks of life and range in age from twelve to forty-nine. They came from the city, country, Mexico, and the military. The fans didn't let a wave of scattered showers stop them from their weekly routine. They mingled outside the grounds, greeting each other with hugs and by name, many old friends from the rodeo circuit.

At Kickers Korner, it's like a family reunion as much as it is a sporting event.

Curtis Murray, a corporal in the National Guard and announcer of two months, sounded like a professional as he blared, "Let's buck some bulls!" to the crowd of more than eighty. "Whenever you're ready, cowboy," he said to Rick Burcham, first in the lineup.

The forty-nine-year-old wrangler had been out of the saddle for three years recovering from personal setbacks. But whatever problems had sidelined him were of little consequence Sunday afternoon. When the cowboys pulled the chute open in the open-air arena, Burcham clenched his rope tight, egged on by fellow riders as he rode like he was in the prime of his career. After his bull pitched him to the dirt, he returned to the maze of fences for a round of congratulatory backslaps from fellow riders for his thrilling go-round.

For Burcham, visions of riding again, albeit in a rodeo for seniors, were starting to look promising. Before the rodeo started, Elgin Tracy, twenty-one, also in the National Guard, kneeled and prayed for strength and forgiveness before jumping on the back of a bull. "I might not get eight seconds," he said, "but I'll give the crowd a hell of a show."

Table Tennis Star Aims for the Top

Lia Morales crouched with her paddle at the ready for a match with Jenson Van Emburgh at the San Antonio Table Tennis Club on the Northeast Side. The eleven-year-old, her eyes focused on the small white ball, stood with her feet wide apart in an attack stance. The hits back and forth were relentless. Lia's parents, Frank and Jeanette Morales, watched from a side bench as she slammed the ball inches across the net, over and over without a miss. After playing the sport for only twenty months, Lia is ranked thirteenth in the country in the girls twelve and under category. She's played in tournaments in Florida and Ohio and at the U.S. nationals in Las Vegas on the Fourth of July.

Every day after school Lia squares off against older, more experienced table tennis players in her quest to become the best of the best. From backhands to forehands, she matched blistering returns from Van Emburgh, twenty-one, who won a bronze medal at the Tokyo 2020 Paralympic Games. A rare miss brought a slight grimace from Lia, but she shook it off and slipped back to her ready stance.

Her coach, Vlad Farcas, twenty-one, kept an eye on the match. Farcas, originally from Romania, also coaches Van Emburgh. In a hushed tone, he offered hints on how to press harder to Lia, a sixth grader at Harlandale Middle School.

Unlike many youngsters, Farcas said, Lia has the rare ability to focus for hours on end. "For her, it's pretty easy because she really likes it a lot. She can play all day. If it were up to her, she would be here 24/7."

Lia has won matches at the club against the older guys who think of her as a little sister, except when they play her at the table. "I like how fast the game is and how difficult it is," she said between matches. "I just try and take what everyone is teaching me and just never give up."

She is currently preparing for a junior tournament in Indiana and her first possible cash prize. She practices for three hours a day, five days a week, at the gym on Lookout Run, which she feels is a second home. Farcas said the gym, a nonprofit, helps people of all levels, including children, adults, seniors, and disabled veterans.

Growing up, Lia dabbled in other activities. The youngest of four children, she's excelled at T-ball, softball, soccer, cheerleading, and competitive dance. Ballet was her focus until she encountered table tennis. She became enamored with the sport when she first saw a table during a visit to the Mission Branch Library with her father.

Oscar Gonzalez, the branch manager and Lia's first coach, taught her the basics at the South Side library near Mission San José. After three weeks Gonzalez told Frank Morales his daughter might be a natural. Gonzalez suggested the youngster go to the San Antonio Table Tennis Club for further development. After one lesson, Farcas asked Morales if he could bring Lia to the club every day.

"She's just picked it up so fast," said Frank Morales, a 1994 graduate of Harlandale High School. "This is what she fell in love with. This is her life. Win or lose, she's hard on herself. She's about making herself better."

At home, Lia watches YouTube videos that send the sound of zipping balls striking tabletops throughout her home. Her parents said the most important thing they want for their daughter is to have fun and be happy. They said she's kept her A-average grades up while rising in the sport. "She's a true blessing," said Jeanette Morales, forty-seven.

During a break in practice last week, Lia sipped lemonade from an orange-and-white-striped cup in an aisle surrounded by several tables where the ricocheting white orbs sounded like hail pelting rooftops in a rainstorm.

"Good job, kiddo," Frank Morales said as she joined him and his wife. "Our job is to congratulate her either way," he said. "We're proud of her."

Toward the end of practice Lia played Kobe Couyoumjian, twenty, who travels from Orange, California, to support his friend Farcas, the players, and the club. The ball was a blur between the two players. She returned almost every ball the tall player sent over the table with a reverse-pendulum serve.

"This game is all about serve and receive," Couyoumjian told Lia and younger players. "If you can get that down, that's most important."

Lia is grateful for her parents' sacrifice and for driving her twenty miles from the South Side to the Northeast Side. She's grateful to her coach and everyone at the gym for the advice she applies to each game. And she plans to carry the lessons from her parents and the club with her into the future.

"I want to make the U.S. national team," she said. "And hopefully, one day bring back a medal from the Olympics."

Keeping Hoop Dreams Alive

As a young girl, Betty Keith was a hoops star. She was so good that folks predicted that she would play basketball after high school, that the sport would take her beyond the cornfields of her hometown of Bernie, Missouri. She had the chance in 1952, when a former coach asked her to try out with the All-American Red Heads, a professional women's basketball team. But her father said no, ending the discussion—and her dream.

Nearly fifty years later the dream was reborn when Keith met Shelly Whitlock at the 1999 Senior Games in Kerrville, where both participated in table tennis. After reminiscing about sinking shots when they were younger, Whitlock asked Keith if she would like to play on a women's basketball team she was starting in Dallas. Keith's childhood dream sputtered to life.

Keith, seventy-three, took her sixty-seven-year-old friend, Rachel Snider, a late-blooming athlete, with her to games in Dallas. Soon after they started playing, the women met another senior athlete, Nellene Pittman, eighty-one, and invited her to join the team.

Today the women are scheduled to play in the Texas Challenge Invitational Playday Tournament in Dallas. "It's wonderful," Snider said. "We're reliving a dream but definitely not moving as fast."

Keith, Snider, and Pittman are the belles of senior women's basketball in San Antonio. They belong to the Texas Challenge, a women's senior basketball league that features a division for women sixty-five and older and one for women eighty-five and older. They regularly drive a hundred miles to Burnet to practice. In the off-season they play several sports at the Jewish Community Center and attend Senior Olympic games.

Earlier this fall the trio took part in a basketball clinic for seniors at Woodlawn Lake Park. Representatives from the Parks and Recreation Department asked Damon Bailey, who played professional basketball in Iceland, to run the clinic. Bailey said the workshop was offered in response to San Antonio being marked as the top city for obesity in some national polls.

"It was a blessed opportunity for me," Bailey said. "I learned so much working with an eighty-one-year-old lady. I have no excuse at twenty-six years old. It's a motivation to see a lady double my age. It's an inspiration."

The women joined several other participants, stretching and doing yoga exercises before running through two hours of drills. They practiced lay-ups, free throws, and passing while running down the court. Off the court, to stay in shape, the women watch what they eat and stay active. Pittman plays tennis and volleyball in city and church leagues. Snider runs twenty-five miles a week and has completed a few marathons. Keith keeps in shape by playing tennis. They said their biggest supporters are their relatives, who buy them athletic gear for Christmas.

They've drawn standing ovations while displaying their basketball skills at WNBA games for the San Antonio Silver Stars and Houston Comets. They want other seniors to see that there isn't anything unusual about playing sports at their age. Their goal now is to gather enough players to form a senior women's basketball team in the Alamo City. "We need people to come join us," Snider said. They should "not be afraid if [they] can't make a basket. They'll learn."

Soccer Play Not Just for Love of the Game

During the early days of Operation Iraqi Freedom, ten-year-old Bakir Ali and his friends kicked soccer balls across cracked tar roads in Baghdad as one-hundred-plus-degree heat faded and darkness cooled the streets. They learned the game from their fathers, practicing near the fortified Green Zone that housed the U.S. Embassy and the Iraqi government. As they grew older, so did their desire grow for the game that lured crowds of men to flickering televisions at sidewalk bars. Echoing bursts of gunfire did little to stop them. They grew savvy, gauging when it was safe to play the game that became their refuge. Fast forward years later to Bakir and other Baghdad boys, now teens, dashing across green fields near the University of Texas Health Science Center, evading challengers and advancing their dreams.

"I grew up with soccer; it's in my blood," Bakir, seventeen, said after a recent game. "Soccer brought us all together."

In 2008 they were among 160 Iraqi refugees who immigrated to San Antonio through the Catholic Charities Refugee Resettlement Program. They cobbled together a squad they call Team Iraqi, following a tradition of immigrants forming soccer teams to preserve their culture.

In America the sport is more than a game for the ten team members, who wear gray T-shirts with numbers written in black marker.

The game also represents a potential pass to a college education and a long-shot audition for a professional team. For Ahmad Hafez, seventeen, the team jokester, it's pure fun. For Adham Nasif, fourteen, the youngest member, it's an introduction to the world's most popular sport. For Bakir, team captain, it's making sure his best friend, Mohammed "Tito" Ibrahim, gets a shot at displaying his talents.

Playing beside his older brothers, Noor and Ibrahim, Tito, eighteen, can pop a soccer ball in the air with his feet, knees, and chest for more than three minutes, just as golfer Tiger Woods did with a golf ball in a Nike commercial. Mostafa Kamal can kick a ball three stories high. A fifteen-year-old sophomore at O'Connor High School, he made the varsity school team and hopes to play his way to a college scholarship.

Five members of the team, including Bakir, played on the O'Connor soccer team last year. "We do this in America to remind us of playing in Iraq," Bakir said after a recent practice. "When we play the game, it's serious."

The teens took to school as they did the game, full force, building on English they already knew. They swerved around a few jibes lobbed their way, moving on, they said, mixing and exchanging cultural practices with American classmates. For the past several months they've piled into the cars of their parents and Pam Espurvoa, a Family Service Association case manager, for rides to their informal practices. "This is a team of young men from Iraq, mostly in high school," Espurvoa said to one of the Americans. "Do you want to play a scrimmage game?"

"They're from where?" the man asked. Then he declined.

"These [kinds of] events make it hard to extend one's hand," Espurvoa said.

Many matches are against players their age from Lebanon, Somalia, Kenya, and Myanmar. In the fall, when a torrential rainstorm threatened to stop a game against a team called the Somali Boys, the teens laughed. Rain was a bonus after years of playing in scorching heat. They squeezed out of three cars, sloshing barefoot onto a water-soaked field, and played.

Recently the Iraqis played the Youngstar Boyz, a group of young Somali men, with the determination of the Lions of Mesopotamia, the national team of Iraq that won the Asian Cup in 2007 and, for a brief period, united Shiites, Sunnis, and Kurds. Weliyo Weliyo, captain of the challengers, refereed the game, which had players' bodies and tempers clashing. Tito bounced balls off his chest, sprinting for a point after teammate Murad Hadad punched the ball to him with his forehead.

Team Iraqi won 4–3. Sometimes they play older teams, such as one formed by Hisham Batar, an assistant director of the Catholic Charities Refugee Resettlement Program. Since Batar, originally from Sudan, arrived in San Antonio in August 2000, he's organized several teams, including a team of refugees in 2003, called Team Unity.

The game has become a bittersweet pastime for two members of Team Iraqi. Tito will age out of any collegiate hopes this year and ponders leaving school to find a job. "My brothers are working and I need to help them too," he said.

Bakir didn't make the school team this year. He has diverted his energy to his studies, but he still wants to open a soccer club one day. "We'll take separate ways," he said, "But we'll always be bonded by soccer."

Young Boxers Take in Lessons at Games of Texas

Wearing a gray sleeveless shirt tucked into long black and silver shorts speckled with black stars, Noah Cardenas stood tall late last week in the corner of a boxing ring, one of more than three hundred young competitive boxers ready to slip punches and jab for glory. His opponent, Roy Rodriguez, sprang from the other corner, swinging. Noah—in the bantam class—snapped straight shots to Rodriguez's head, popping it back. Rodriguez responded with overhand swings. "Back him up, back him up," yelled Noah's trainer, Santo "Sam" Randazzo.

Noah stepped forward, delivering the blows he had practiced for six months. Then the bell sounded, ending the last round. The ten-year-old boxer was one of thousands of junior Olympic athletes who participated in the 2009 Games of Texas, a multisport event. Held at various venues across the city, boxing is one of sixteen sports sponsored by San Antonio Sports and the San Antonio Parks and Recreation Department and patterned after the Olympic Games. Before the match between Noah and Roy began at Woodlawn Gymnasium, Randazzo threaded white tape in and around Noah's fingers.

"The kids are like veterans," said Randazzo, who trains the boy at his Northeast Side gym and called the event a tune-up for young boxers across the city and state. "This is where the De La Hoyas come from."

The match was Noah's second bout ever. He became interested in the sport after hanging out with his best friend and his father, a former boxer. Noah's father, Dan Cardenas, said his son—who weighs sixty-three pounds and reaches four feet, eight inches—lost his first fight but never went down. "He came out of it with ideas of his own to do things different next time," Cardenas said. "I was happy with that."

Minutes before the fight, Noah sat alone, counting on his training to settle his nerves. "When I'm in there, it's like practice," he said. "It reminds me of hitting the pads and what my coach tells me."

The third match of the day, Noah and Rodriguez doubled their pace in the last round, both looking for an edge. At the last clang of the bell Noah flicked his lean arm out as Randazzo shouted, "Work the jab, Noah, work the jab!" As the crowd waited for the score, Noah walked across the canvas and shook hands with his opponent's trainer. He then thanked his opponent for a good fight. Then the judge stood between the boys.

The announcer spoke—Rodriguez had won by decision. Noah looked to his corner, his mouth open. His father pulled him to his chest and rubbed his curly hair.

Noah left the ring with his father, having earned another lesson from a sport where opponents still cross the ring and congratulate each other for a fine effort.

Texas Bad Boys

For the past few weeks a cluster of youngsters has scrimmaged on a parched East Side field as part of an annual rite of fall—youth football. They play for the Texas Bad Boys, started by Kashif Tibbs, an advocate of youth sports and a former coach for other sports organizations.

Called Coach K.T. by his players, he has created a free, independent football program for East Side kids ages four to twelve who might not be able to afford to play in private leagues. He has several coaches, teen moms, and cheerleading directors—all volunteers—supporting his effort. It's a good idea, but Tibbs is facing serious challenges, including lack of resources. Still, these youngsters aren't deterred.

"These kids are so important. I can't break their hearts," Tibbs, twenty-nine, said. "They're expecting to play; failure isn't an option."

The team plays in the North American Junior Independent Football Federation in four classes: flag, ages four to six; freshman, ages seven and eight; junior varsity, ages nine and ten; and varsity, ages eleven and twelve. Their first game is scheduled in a few weeks against the San Antonio Beast, but they need helmets and shoulder pads. The team missed the first date when they could've practiced in pads and uniforms a week or so ago because they didn't have money to get the equipment. They started a GoFundMe page for donations.

Tibbs's two sons play for the team, and he's also recruited about thirty girls from ages three to fourteen as cheerleaders. The day after his third son was born earlier this month, Tibbs was back on the field. His wife, Ashley, said he supported her, and now it's time to help him realize his dream. "He's real passionate about this," she said. "It's all he talks about."

Recently, as older players ran through drills, one of the coaches, Keith Scott, worked with nine tykes, each barely as tall as a fire hydrant, on the rules of flag football. His biggest challenge was keeping the easily distracted little ones in the huddle.

"Y'all got to pay attention," Scott, thirty-four, said as he coaxed them into their stances. "The way you practice is the way you'll play in a game."

There weren't enough balls, so Scott improvised, grabbing a plastic bottle half-filled with blue Gatorade from the grass. He egged the lively youngsters on as they tucked in the bottle-turned-football, ran with gusto, and scored imaginary touchdowns.

Mount Sinai Baptist Church has stepped in to help. Tibbs's friend LeMoure "B.U." Stephens is working with supporters from Dallas to help provide equipment. "He's doing a great thing," said Stephens, cofounder of Shooting Stars Sports and Entertainment. "A lot of kids need what he's providing."

Tibbs has sought advice from old football coaches and community leaders, including Taj Matthews, executive director of the Claude & ZerNona Black Developmental Leadership Foundation. "When I see someone go out on faith for our kids, I'm behind them 100 percent," Matthews said.

To the kids, Tibbs is part drill sergeant, guru, and counselor, who stresses discipline and structure. He's big on manners for the players, such as saying "sir" and "ma'am" when they answer adults. And as part of the program, he sees that they get to church on Sundays.

Tibbs grew up on the East Side without his father, who has been in prison for twenty-two years, but he said he had coaches who taught him life skills he still follows. He wants to do the same for his players and his sons. "They see the facade of things and temptations that can change your life if you bite into it. It's so easy to do wrong and hard to do right. I want to help them make choices."

Across the field, boys who didn't listen when a coach was talking were doing push-ups. Jamarion Clark, eleven, ran through drills with Xavier Beck, twelve; Donavan Beal, nine; and David Jones, ten. All were focused on repetitions.

Clark doesn't have a problem with Tibbs's no-nonsense rules. "It makes us stronger," he said. "He wants us to do good and not give up. When we do bad stuff, we know there are consequences."

Saul Peña sat in a folding lawn chair watching his sons, Dominic, eleven, and Isaiha, eight, sprint across the field. Peña's boys work out for two hours at the Calderon Boxing Gym before football practice. "It keeps them out of trouble," he said. "I want them to grow up to be disciplined."

When practice ended, Tibbs led the group in the Lord's Prayer and after a collective "amen" it was time to shake off the sweat and release a little self-affirming energy.

"Texas Bad Boys, what time is it?" Tibbs yelled.

"It's time to get loud! It's time to represent!" the boys shouted in response. "We're the Texas Bad Boys! We're them Bad Boys—we're so good, we're Bad Boys!"

Fighting One More Bout

The bell rang on the budding boxer's amateur career when his opponent's bleeding nose turned the amateur's white shoes red. After the blood splattered on Jose Luis Alvarez, he pulled back on delivering haymakers and lost the match in a decision in the 108-pound class at the 2012 San Antonio Golden Gloves. But the defeat didn't affect his confidence.

Outside the ring at the Woodlawn Gym, Alvarez was still a champion. He had won forty-five medals in the academic decathlon arena at Edison High School and was bound for Our Lady of the Lake University. The teen had an industrious drive that stemmed from life lessons his single mother taught him, coupled with the faith of two men who invested in his athletic and educational endeavors. But he harbored a secret. He wasn't here legally.

Some four years later, buoyed by his mom and other supporters, he walked across the stage at Freeman Coliseum to receive his bachelor's degree in accounting.

"I reminisce about my past and where I come from. I could have not been here," Alvarez, twenty-one, said. "I could have not been in college or maybe not in the United States. I'm very grateful to be in the place I am."

He was two months old when his mother brought him from

Mexico to San Antonio for surgery on his scalp. She raised him in a South Side home, where she rose at 4 a.m. to go to work and earn a wage to provide for him. In high school he wanted something to alleviate the stress of studying and began boxing at Jesse James Leija's ChampionFit Gym. After training at the gym after school, he'd head back to the classroom, and from 7 to 8 p.m. he practiced for the decathlon. Leija learned about his achievements at school and introduced the quiet, focused teen to another boxer at the gym, Roy Terracina, chairman of Our Lady of the Lake's board of trustees. He encouraged the teen to apply to the university. Alvarez was accepted and the university covered most of his costs, with other scholarships taking care of his remaining tuition.

Terracina recommended Alvarez for an internship and bought him suits to wear on the job. His supervisors called him one of their hardest workers. Despite Alvarez's accomplishments, Terracina noticed that a heavy burden seemed to be weighing on him. When he asked what was bothering him, however, the young man hesitated.

He hesitated because he didn't have residential status and was worried about his future. He couldn't talk about it, and he often wondered whether his hard work would be for naught. Then, in his sophomore year, he applied for the national Deferred Action for Childhood Arrivals program and secured a two-year work permit that allows him to stay in the United States legally.

Implemented in 2012, the program grants two-year work permits to some undocumented immigrants who arrived in the United States as young children and have lived here ever since. The program was to be expanded in February 2015 but was stopped by a Texas-led lawsuit that is awaiting a decision by the U.S. Supreme Court.

For now, at least, Alvarez has legal status. "It was a big relief to attain it," he said of the permit, choking up. "That got me motivated to continue on, because I was able to help my family."

The chairman saw a vision of himself in Alvarez. Terracina came from the Chicago inner city and was a prize fighter at a young age. "I couldn't be prouder of this young man," Terracina, sixty-nine, said. "This kid is just a feel-good story for me."

After Alvarez's internship at the BDO USA San Antonio office, he will work full-time for the company. Boxing helped set him on the road to success, making him more outgoing and giving him hope.

"I thought at the very least, if nothing ends up happening at school, I can box," he said. "I felt if I could do this, I could do anything. Luckily, I didn't have to, [but] it really changed my life."

Breaking Barriers and Records

Before they broke records on tracks across the city, state, and nation, the youngest and middle Glosson brothers raced each other in a side yard of their one-story home on Burnet Street. Their grandfather would give the two skinny boys a countdown. Ed Glosson usually flew out front, holding the lead in the twenty-yard run. A length of their mother's sewing thread served as the finish line. Ed's older brother Clyde would stew after each loss.

"What are you getting mad about?" their grandfather would ask. "If you want to win, get better."

That's what Clyde did. The sibling competition helped all three Glosson brothers. Ed, Clyde, and the late Julius Glosson, the oldest, were among standout athletes in San Antonio public schools in the mid-1960s and, later, in collegiate and professional sports.

Ed and Clyde attended Phillis Wheatley High School, an all-Black school that closed in 1970. Julius was so good that he was recruited by other high schools and attended Brackenridge and Highlands. Wheatley was part of the Prairie View Interscholastic League, which oversaw extracurricular activities of the state's African American public schools. The league produced such athletic legends as football linemen Bubba Smith, "Mean" Joe Greene, and Tody Smith; wide receivers Otis Taylor, Cliff Branch, and Jerry

LeVias; quarterback Eldridge Dickey; and heavyweight fighter George Foreman.

The Black league merged with the University Interscholastic League in 1967. Ed Glosson played running back and defensive back in the state's first integrated public school football game, against Kerrville's Tivy High School before fourteen thousand people at Alamo Stadium. He recalled his coaches telling him and his teammates that it wasn't about Black or white but about holding their own in a new league.

"You didn't realize the importance at the time," Ed Glosson, now seventy, said in a recent interview. "But now you look back, and we were at the right place at the right time. We just liked to compete. We never felt like we were second class."

The Glosson brothers' names are engraved on state championship plaques and in national record books. Ed and Clyde say their success in track and football wouldn't have been possible without lessons learned in their East Side community and at Wheatley.

"Our teachers told us we couldn't play football or run track all of our lives," said Clyde, seventy-two, and an ordained minister, noting that athletes were encouraged to focus on academics as well as sports at Wheatley. "No one can take your education from you."

Barry Robinson, a former *San Antonio Express-News* sports editor, said the Glosson brothers are forever linked to an era of great San Antonio athletes. He called Wheatley a powerhouse of champions who opened the eyes of college recruiters to talent across the city. "You could not ignore their incredible athletic ability, their speed and agility," Robinson said of the Glossons. "They set the stage for all of that to happen."

Recently the two brothers reminisced at Ed's home on the East Side about belonging to the city's premier class of high school athletes. Clyde's daughter, Dana Glosson Barnes, herself a former track star and coach, said she knows her family's resume well.

"My dad taught me that if you're going to do it, you're going to do it right," she said. "You will uphold yourself with honor and respect at all times."

The Glosson brothers' teachers and coaches expected the boys' best efforts in the classroom and on the field. And they followed their mother's simple creed: don't quit. Those points were driven home by their Wheatley football and track coach, Henry Carroll, a disciplinarian who treated starters and bench warmers the same. When his young charges' efforts were lacking during practice, he kept them working late into the night, relying on the headlights of parked cars.

Clyde would go on to achieve national titles as a sprinter at Trinity University, participate in the 1968 Olympic trials, and play pro ball with the Chiefs and the Buffalo Bills. After his stint with the NFL, he taught for twenty-seven years in San Antonio Independent School District.

While there didn't seem to be much racism in their neighborhood growing up, Clyde recalled encountering overt racial outbursts at competitions outside of San Antonio. There was the time his track team was confronted by an angry crowd in Midland. Their driver pulled up to a hamburger stand, and several men surrounded the thirteen-year-old and his teammates with sticks and bats. A woman from the area defused the situation, telling the crowd to leave the boys alone. Minutes later the team directed its focus back to the upcoming meet, Clyde recalled. It's a tale he relates to youngsters about the attitudes of the era.

"If you're not careful, history can repeat itself," daughter Barnes said. "If you are not preparing yourself to do better, you will be back in a situation you never thought you would be in."

Ed graduated from the University of Missouri with a bachelor's degree in journalism. He worked at the *San Antonio Light* for several years as a general assignment reporter, winning regional and state awards. In 1979 he bought the *San Antonio Register*, a Black newspaper, from publisher Valmo Bellinger. The most difficult story he ever wrote, he said, was the account of his brother Julius's murder in 1983. Ed said he was in tears as he went against his mother's wishes in reporting how Julius's girlfriend shot him in the back outside an East Side home.

Clyde said he and Ed would like to gather their old sports friends and have an annual summit in San Antonio to teach kids the lessons their teachers and coaches taught them. It's the same lessons they have passed on to Barnes and her sons and to Ed's children: Jennifer Allen, Edwin Glosson, Lauren Glosson Fairley, and Evan Glosson. Clyde said all youngsters need to hear that they can become doctors, lawyers, or whatever else they want to be.

"We have to teach them to find their gift," the reverend said. "And we need to tell them they are special. That's what our teachers told us."

Bunco Club Makes Its Final Roll of the Dice

For many years there were days when the chatter inside Mildred Hartman's house blared like a baseball catcher badgering a batter to swing. There was the sound of clattering dice, yellowed and worn from years of use, rolling across folding tables. There was the rustling of hands, etched with age, that slipped away with each roll of the dice. And there was the ringing of a black-handled bell that sparked the action.

"Dingle it," Sylvia Philips, eighty-seven, says as Hartman clangs the bell signaling a round of bunco games.

Hartman's partner, Lillian Levis, ninety-three, rubs the dice between her palms as if sprinkling spice over a pot of boiling soup. She spins the dice onto the table, twirling, tumbling, and teetering on winning numbers that never seem to stop.

"Lillian, you're hot," Hartman says. "You're hot as a baked potato."

Levis's eyes stay fixed on the three cubes scattering from her hands. The only audience is Hartman's smiling relatives, looking on from framed photos hung on surrounding living room walls. "Two more, girl," Hartman says as Levis racks up nineteen points. "You got it made. Those last two points are the hardest to get."

"That's enough already, Lillie!" Philips, a member of the other team, says, eyeing Levis. "I think I'll take a nap."

Levis shakes two consecutive rolls that end the thirteenth game of the afternoon.

"Twenty-one!" Hartman yells, ringing the bell. "How about that?"

The rattling of dice among close friends has been a constant in Levis's life. She was twenty-three years old when she first joined her friends every third Thursday of the month for good conversation, a bit of food, and an afternoon of bunco games. Seventy years later it's getting physically harder for Levis and other members to get up and around.

"It's just too much effort to get together," Levis says. "I'd like to go longer, but it's just too much on me."

Levis was one of thirteen women who took up the parlor game to socialize while their husbands worked and their children went to school. Now there are eight. Levis is the last original member. It's the last game of the Bunco Ladies Club.

They started playing at the end of the Great Depression, running three tables where camaraderie and friendship grew. They ran carpools to pick up members from different parts of town. It was a time when toddlers amused themselves by playing ball and romping outside all day. Hobos rode the rails and minimum wage was forty cents an hour. Mexican female pecan-shellers went on strike in downtown San Antonio for better pay. Walt Disney's *Snow White and the Seven Dwarfs* was the highest-grossing film of the decade. Heavyweight boxer Joe Louis knocked out Max Schmeling before seventy thousand spectators in Yankee Stadium.

Each month a different woman played hostess. She'd make a lunch of her choice that included light finger food and salads. The meals grew larger; members chuckled, as each woman tried to top the last offering. As they reached their sixties, the work became too much, and they dined at restaurants before their games.

Their children caught onto the game early, listening as their mothers played in other rooms and craning their necks to watch as the action rolled. Levis's daughter, Lorraine Green, filled in for missing members as she grew older. She knows the women and history of the club as well as any of the members. She carries on skills she learned from her mother in her own bunco club.

Hartman's daughter, Kay Clifton, forty-nine, remembers the bunco games from the time she first could walk. She thought it was cool when she became a teen and her mother let her sub for an absent member. Clifton stopped by with her nineteen-year-old daughter, Michelle, to help Hartman, a sixty-three-year member, serve the last round of dessert and coffee.

"It's all about gossip and fun," Clifton says, watching the women say their goodbyes. "It's kind of sad to see it end."

They're all widows except for one. They've mourned several original members' passing and attended the funerals of each other's spouses. Moving from table to table was their exercise. In recent years members called and reminded each other of games. They called each other "country" or "city" girls, depending on where they lived and how far the city limits of the day reached. And they say it was the births, deaths, loves, and triumphs that brought them closer and made them stronger.

"We love and respect each other," Leona H. Finger says. "We've always been there for each other through all of the tragedies. We never had cross words, but we might have slapped someone if they tried to grab a bunco."

After the final throw of the dice they sip coffee, munch on Hartman's cherry scramble dump cake, and step up to claim prizes that range from five dollars down to one dollar. They take off different colored bunco cards hanging around their necks, perforated with punched holes for their wins. They rub each other's hands and promise to phone each other before they leave. They kiss each other's cheeks and walk out in pairs to cars filling Hartman's driveway.

Now they'll while away the third Thursday of each month in other ways. Some will continue playing with other groups. Some will play solitaire, do crossword puzzles, and comb through the memories of the afternoons they spent together. They'll all have memories of Hartman egging on Levis, who counted her points as she blistered the table one last time.

"Oh, you haven't lost your touch at all," Hartman said as Levis scooped up the dice with one swipe. "We got a hot one over here."

"Who?" a player from the other table asked.

"Lillian," Hartman says. "She's going out in a blaze of glory."

DANCE HALLS, ELVIS, AND SOUNDS OF SOUL

Old-School Dances at South Side Ballroom

Everyone has a dance partner at the Royal Palace Ballroom, where the music always has an old-school spin. The dance hall at 3506 Southwest Military Drive is a revered South Side spot, where older San Antonians—and some younger folk—go for camaraderie and companionship Sunday through Thursday afternoons.

Retired and current musicians play songs that draw retirees, veterans, widows, and widowers en masse across a dimly lit dance floor. Fedoras and Stetsons cast shadows on the men's brows. Multicolored lights shimmer on the women's hair, swept up in swirls and curls. And it doesn't matter if the beat is fast or slow; the couples circle the floor, hands clasped in the air, lost in the conjunto rhythms.

Nearly forty years ago Eusebio "Chevo" Garcia and Jose Gonzales Jr. opened the dance hall to offer older residents a place to gather at a time when senior venues were in short supply. In addition to being a mainstay for elders, it's also a popular spot for weddings and special events. Most often, Gonzales, now eighty, can be found in the kitchen/bar serving patrons. A table is still reserved for Garcia, who died in 2006.

Now Garcia's daughter, Rosie Herrera, manages the dance hall along with her brother, Jose Garcia. They also have help from their siblings, Eusebio Garcia Jr., Maria Alma Teniente, Alice Rodriguez, and Susie Martinez.

"It's been a traditional thing since my father and Mr. Gonzales started it," Herrera said. "It's homegrown."

Jose Garcia credited his mother, Dolores, for raising him and his siblings with business sense. He said she ran the photography agency, Royal Studios, and helped his father finance the ballroom. The music still has the same beat, but there have been changes. Admission was one dollar; now patrons pay two.

To honor her patrons' loyalty, Herrera created Las Vegas Night, Senior Prom, and the popular coronation of royal ambassadors. The seniors elect royalty who serve for a year as Queen, Princess, Sweetheart, and Fiesta King. Queen Rose Sotelo, seventy, handed out candy, flowers, and fans to garner votes in early May. She said that during her reign she plans to stay in touch with her ballroom friends.

"And if they don't come, I'll call them and see why," Sotelo said as couples filled the dance floor, slow dancing to the sounds of Los Veteranos.

Susie Martinez said that today's customers stop by for their health as well as fellowship.

"More seniors are living longer," she said. "They come and dance for the exercise."

Hector S. Castro, sixty-seven, has been a regular at the dance hall for eighteen years. He knows the names and histories of the seniors who congregate at the long tables framing the dance floor. He said the dance hall is a place where folks can catch up on each other's lives, make new friends, and, sometimes, find more than a dance partner.

That was the case for Gloria and Felipe Zuriata. Four years ago they were both widowed. When the band struck up "Corazón de Oro," or "Heart of Gold," Felipe Zuriata asked Gloria for a dance beneath white lights dangling from the ceiling like parched grapevines.

After three meetings, he asked her to marry him. They never dated, Gloria Zuriata said. They just took a chance.

"It was a good chance," she said. "I was tired of being alone. It's ugly. Just because we're seniors doesn't mean our life is ending. We're just beginning."

Soul Still in His Heart

In 1975 a band from San Antonio strode into a downtown soul club in Fort Worth to face a scene that played out wherever they appeared. The owner, an older, burly Black man, asked for the lead singer. The Black musicians pointed to Roger Gonzalez, a Latino.

"Aw, hell," the owner said. "This ain't going to work!"

But Gonzalez just smiled as the big man frowned. The band stepped on the dimly lit stage. Building with unstoppable power, the Latino's gritty voice poured out the deep passion of Luther Ingram's "If Loving You Is Wrong, I Don't Want to Be Right" and Billy Paul's "Me and Mrs. Jones." Couples hit the floor, clenching each other in slow-dance moves. At the end of the set, the club owner bulled his way through the crowd and headed straight for Gonzalez. "You," he said, "you're one of us."

For more than fifty years Gonzalez's raw, soulful voice has convinced skeptics that he's the real thing. On the Chitlin' Circuit, through Texas, Louisiana, and Mississippi, word of his talent and repertoire spread as he performed with groups of the era that included the Rhythm Kings, the Marvells, and the Soul Makers.

One recent morning, he sat in a McDonald's downtown near Frio Street, spinning the story of his life as, outside, day laborers clamored around contractors' trucks for jobs.

"The Lord cut me that way," Gonzalez said of singing soul music. "I never shied away from it; I took it as a great challenge."

In the 1970s he sang at Johnnie Phillips's Eastwood Country Club with bands that opened for famous Black artists such as Ike and Tina Turner, Etta James, and B. B. King. In the 1980s he sang in Tejano bands, notably with Zapata, which opened for Malo of Suavecito fame at the Municipal Auditorium. Gonzalez, sixty-five, is a recipient of the Randy Award, named for musician Randy Garibay, one of his biggest inspirations. During his career he rode the highs and lows of show business. He slept on floors and plush beds, traveled in cramped Cadillacs and vans. After shows he sipped the always available liquor, falling into years of alcoholism that threatened to still his voice.

Gonzalez's career has its roots in the mid-1960s when, as a student at Edison High School, Little Richard and James Brown drew him to soul and the blues. He stepped out front when he subbed for a sick lead singer and never looked back. In 1968 the members of Los Keys named him Little Roger because of his small stature. His mother became his biggest fan, but in his fledgling days, much to her chagrin, he didn't sing Spanish songs; he sang tunes that popped like grease in a hot skillet and told tales of wronged lovers.

When he stepped onstage, many Black crowds were taken aback—until they heard him sing. As he walked off the stage one night, a woman stopped him and said, "Little Roger, you're just a Black man wrapped in a brown man's body."

Not everyone was enamored of Little Roger. There were a number of close calls in Mississippi. In 1975 he was playing in Laurel with the Marvells, featuring a Black drummer and three white musicians, when members of the Ku Klux Klan threatened the band. The standoff ended when the white owner stood up for his performers.

The pinnacle of his career was at the Eastwood. One night Bobby

"Blue" Bland's valet said Bland wanted to see him. Nervous, Gonzalez followed the towering man to the singer's dressing room.

Bland just stared at him, then asked, "Are you Little Roger, the guy that was singing?"

"Yes, sir," he said.

The blues singer told Gonzalez that he liked his voice but hadn't expected a Mexican American to walk through the door. "That was an honor," Gonzalez said. "It was like I made the full circle."

Music critic Jim Beal said Bland's comment attested to Gonzalez's talent.

"At that time, there was no bigger seal of approval. That was all the validation anybody would need. That was better than *America's Got Talent* or *The Voice*—that was Bobby Bland."

Beal said Gonzalez had what it took to make his name in a predominately Black world. "He had enough gall to go out and do that," he said of Gonzalez singing soul. "That was the mark of a lot of West Side R&B guys. He had the confidence and knowledge that he could do the job if hired."

But endless traveling to gigs and the fast-paced world of nightclubs were Gonzalez's downfall. For eleven years he drank a fifth of whiskey daily. The gigs slowed, then stopped. To earn a living, he turned to booking acts at neighborhood clubs and working as a mechanic. He got divorced; he has a son and a daughter. They didn't follow his musical path.

His mother, a born-again Christian, prayed for Jesus to take the bottle out of his hand. "I'm going to pray for you, son," she said, "because you are in a bad way."

In 1982 her prayers came true. One morning Gonzalez was at her house and found that he couldn't take another swig. He asked to be free of his addiction. He's now been sober for twenty-eight years. He hasn't gone back to the stellar heights of his youth, but he still performs at venues around San Antonio with his trademark viselike grip on the microphone.

And he's passing on life lessons to younger players, such as twenty-seven-year-old guitarist Will Owen Gage, who has been playing with local blues bands since he was eleven. Gonzalez has played with Gage's trio, and Gage said he's planning to have Gonzalez as the featured player on a regular basis. The younger bluesman said Gonzalez and other soul survivors, such as Arturo "Sauce" Gonzalez and the West Side Horns, deserve more attention from the public.

"These guys didn't push me away when I was cutting my teeth," he said. "San Antonio is a music town with guys like Roger who have been around since the 1960s and beyond. People need to hear Little Roger. If any man gets the blues, it's Little Roger."

Living the King's Dream

He has strolled in every weekday for the past five years, leaving a slight stir in his wake. Patrons stare as the man with the flipped collar and slick pompadour heads to a corner table in the back of Eddie's Taco House on Cevallos Street. His posse of one—Maria, his wife of thirty years—follows closely. After all this time, she's used to the stares. Lunchtime diners gaze at her husband's four-inch gold collar, studded with colorful penny-sized rhinestones, fastened to his black shirt with metal paper holders. They gaze at the rustic chain belt that loops through his black pants and the epaulets, with square, metallic studs, that rest on his slight shoulders. Gold-rimmed sunglasses shield his eyes as he takes in the attention. Some customers whisper about the pompadour that flows to his neck, curling into a ducktail over the collar. They do the same about the pair of thick lamb-chop sideburns that plaster his jaws. And before he's settled in his chair, it's likely that someone will utter a phrase that sums up his visit: "The King's back!"

In homage to the King of Rock 'n' Roll, Juan Manuel Quintanilla adopted Elvis Presley's fashion style several years ago. It's a style that his father, Antonio Quintanilla, forbade him from wearing when he was alive. He honored his father's wishes and dressed like an average guy. But after his father died, Quintanilla slipped on the garb of the man whose cool music thrilled him as a teen. No longer does he reach for an average pair of jeans or a T-shirt. Indeed, every day he wakes up and clothes himself in Elvis-inspired costumes.

"They call me Elvis. I don't say nothing," said the slender fifty-eight-year-old, leaning back in his chair and surveying the eatery that serves his favorite food. "But I like it. It makes me feel good."

He isn't alone. There are thousands of people around the world just like him who wrap themselves in the persona of the rockabilly icon. They span all descriptions, defying age, size, race, and creed. Quintanilla doesn't belong to a fan club, but he carries a folded, faded picture of Elvis in his wallet beneath a laminated copy of Presley's driver's license.

Though he dresses out of the ordinary, Quintanilla seems to have reached the highest stage of self-actualization, said Elizabeth Stanczak, executive director of health and counseling services at the University of Texas at San Antonio. Self-actualization is at the top of noted behavioral psychologist Abraham Maslow's list of essential needs. Others include physical, safety, social, and esteem needs.

"He's basically living out something denied as a young person but giving back to the community in an uncontroversial way," she said. "How much better can life get that strangers smile because of what you're wearing."

Stanczak said Quintanilla isn't hurting anyone and is aware of his own identity. "Dressing as his hero has allowed him a way to live his dream in a positive way."

Yet with all the Elvis look-alikes populating the land, heads still turn when Quintanilla arrives at his favorite lunch spot. The staff at Eddie's isn't bothered by any hoopla when he enters the room. They know when he's due to arrive at the eatery and are poised to place his usual order. Unlike Presley, it's not a banana and peanut butter sandwich but rather a bean and chorizo breakfast taco, even at the noon hour. Manager Priscilla Caballero said customers enjoy the effort Quintanilla puts into his wardrobe. "It's great having him here."

Customers Roger de la Cruz, René Palacios, and Ernest Martinez have met for lunch at the café for the past five years and have yet to approach Quintanilla. The friends respect his privacy but are curious about his appearance. "We never see him in street clothes like us," de la Cruz said. "We've always wondered. We're thinking about taking a picture with him."

Since Quintanilla converted to his alter ego, hundreds of passersby have asked for his photo. They've snapped his picture while shopping at Walmart and H-E-B and stopped in his car at a red light. He is also the subject of stares and conversation at a restaurant on Pleasanton Road he frequents every Saturday night.

Maria Quintanilla, fifty-one, said their five children, ranging in age from twenty to thirty-one, approve of his choice in clothes. His latest project is the ultimate Elvis must-have—a replica of the famous white Aloha suit, complete with a cape to the hip and flaring bell-bottoms.

Quintanilla is content wearing his Elvis-inspired wardrobe but said he's had thoughts of branching out to the King's music. As a teen he played the bajo sexto guitar at local spots with his brother Oscar, who played the accordion. They recruited another brother and friend and toured the region as a quartet. Today, two pinched discs hinder Quintanilla from playing instruments with his right hand, but he said his voice is fine. These days he's practicing five of Presley's hits, trying them out for size.

"If people like it," he said, sipping sweet tea from a straw jutting from a large glass, "I could get an act together."

An Army Photo with Elvis

When Larry Lupear thinks of Elvis Presley, it's not as the "King of Rock 'n' Roll" but as a fellow soldier he trained and served with. And he has a photo taken more than sixty years ago on a U.S. Army post in West Germany to prove it. Lupear, a retired auto executive who now lives in San Antonio, was eighteen at the time; Presley was twenty-three. Lupear was from Detroit; Presley was from Tupelo, Mississippi. They came from different backgrounds and their lives would take different paths, but in the army they were both soldiers.

In 1958 the army drafted Presley at the height of his fame. The music idol, whose gyrations caused teenage girls to swoon and parents to seethe, became one of the thousands of the army's newly inducted soldiers. Lupear first met the star in basic training at Fort Hood, and they saw each other a few times there. Months later they would serve together in Company D, 32nd Tank Battalion, 3rd Armored Division, posted at Friedberg, Germany.

Lupear recalls standing in line at the post exchange in Friedberg, unaware that the soldier in front of him was the man of "Jailhouse Rock" fame. Then he saw the stunned look on the cashier's face. Lupear recalled that Presley turned around and jokingly said, "Boy, it would be good to get some help around here, wouldn't it?" They laughed, shook their heads, and caught up with each other's lives. Presley walked outside and was instantly mobbed.

While sitting in a jeep on guard duty, Lupear asked Presley if he would sign an autograph for his sister. Presley did more than that; he signed some thirty pages of a small spiral notebook for him. Lupear has heard estimates that one single autograph could be worth $1,500, but he said money wasn't what interested him then or now. In fact, he doesn't know where the autographed pages ended up, but the photo a buddy took of him and Presley in uniform has a place of prominence on a shelf in Lupear's living room. "It was just a cool, interesting thing in my life," he said. "I got to know him. He was a pretty down-to-earth guy. He just wanted to be a regular Joe."

Whenever they saw each other, it was without fanfare, the retired General Motors manager, now eighty, said; Presley never talked about stardom or the show business side of his life. They were just soldiers hanging out, jawing about topics that matter in the lives of young soldiers everywhere: girls, family, military life.

Presley didn't live in the barracks but off post with his father and friends from Memphis. Still, he and Lupear saw each other occasionally. Lupear recalled how devastated Presley was after his mother died. She was just forty-six. And he remembered when Presley brought Priscilla Beaulieu, the fourteen-year-old daughter of an air force colonel to a dance. Chaperones were present, but there weren't any displays of affection between the famous soldier and the teen he would marry in 1967.

After his 1958–60 army commitment, Presley went back to the glitz and glamour of Hollywood. There were a few phone calls to his army buddy, Lupear remembers, but the lines of communication faded as each man moved on with his life. Lupear separated from the military after six years with an honorable discharge. He worked a series of jobs that included his father's tool and die shop. He served as a law enforcement officer and later as a manager at General Motors.

Fifteen years after leaving the army, Lupear saw Priscilla again during a General Motors luncheon in Dallas. "I've got to tell you something," he said. "I met you a long time ago." When he told her about the dance, they laughed and reminisced about life at the army post.

Through the years, Lupear watched his old friend's life play out across his television screen. There was the soaring rise of fame with TV specials, albums, and concerts. He watched as popular music and culture eclipsed his friend, who was burdened by divorce, drugs, and weight gain. And then came August 16, 1977, the day Presley died of heart failure at Graceland.

"It just didn't look like him," Lupear said. "I felt so bad. He was like his momma's boy. He loved his mother, and when she passed away he kind of went to hell."

Lupear retired in San Antonio in 1997, more than 5,300 miles from the post in West Germany where he hung out and snapped a treasured photo with Elvis. But he almost lost the photo when he put up his house for sale.

One day his realtor suggested he keep a closer eye on his memento and handed it to him. The agent had just retrieved it from a woman who had taken it off a wall and tried to put it in her purse. Now the one-of-a-kind portrait sits above rows of pristine model cars parked on bookshelves in Lupear's North Side home. Many viewers look at the picture and see a son of Detroit standing beside a historic figure. When he looks at the framed photo, all he sees is two regular Joes. And he smiles.

Playlists Still Sound Great, Static or Not

The music hummed to life with the turn of a knob. In the late 1960s I listened to tunes of the trying times—soul, pop, and rock—on a chocolate brown RCA radio, 1950s vintage, handed down from my great-grandparents. Clear vacuum tubes glowed like the day's first light, visible through slots in the back of the hard Bakelite cover. The sound was scrambled through static until it was fine-tuned and clear on the AM dial.

Listening to the hits on KAPE and KTSA was a daily ritual when I lived off Five Palms Drive, near Lackland Air Force Base. Marvin Gaye addressed an unfaithful lover and bet she wondered how he knew in his version of "Heard It through the Grapevine." Jose Feliciano's rendition of the Doors' "Light My Fire" blistered through the speaker. The Beatles advised us we could take a sad song and make it better in "Hey Jude."

Today they're classics. At the time they were among the many that made up the soundtrack of our lives. Thanks to my mother, I grew up on a steady diet of music and reading, not necessarily in that order. Books and magazines rivaled the albums and 45s that took up space in our living room.

At the dawn of the 1970s, we moved to Omaha, Nebraska. The clear tubes glowed one last time, and then the old radio stayed behind. There was still the one in the car. Tommy James and the

Shondells crooned "Crystal Blue Persuasion" along many of the nine hundred miles up Interstate 35 from Texas to the Cornhusker State. We arrived in North Omaha as social commentary wafted along the radio waves. Having graduated from the hulk of a tube radio to a sardine can–size transistor radio with collapsible antenna, I first heard James Taylor's "Fire and Rain" and Sir Elton John's "Your Song" on that silver-faced, battery-powered box, snug in the pocket of a winter coat. From time to time, the screaming guitar of Santana's "Black Magic Woman" pulsed through the earbud.

Barbra Streisand sang for her mother to save her from the "Stoney End," as we encountered our first swirling, white-out blizzard. In seventh and eighth grade I met Lonzale Ramsey, Willie Richardson, and Fred Montgomery. We all connected over the chorus of the times.

"The music had a sense of unity for us, Black people and people as a whole," Richardson said. "To me, there's nothing like R&B. It was just good music that bonded you together. Sometimes we didn't have money to do a lot of things, but we could get together and listen to music. That's the power the music had."

We dissected the messages of Gaye's opus, "What's Going On," an album in heavy rotation that called to end war, save the environment, and pray for the inner city. Aretha Franklin's "Amazing Grace" echoed through screen doors throughout the neighborhood. Curtis Mayfield's "Back to the World" added a refrain about the hard times of the era.

Each time the Temptations' psychedelic soul hit "Ball of Confusion" played, we'd tick off the chaotic list that still seems relevant. We gravitated to songs that spun a story, like Stevie Wonder's "Living for the City," a sorrowful tale of a boy's doomed escape from poverty in Mississippi to New York City, where a street scam lands him in jail.

We each had a theme song. Lonzale's was the Four Tops' "Are You Man Enough." Willie's was Graham Central Station's "Can You

Handle It." Fred's was "Big John" by Rare Earth. Mine, also by Rare Earth, was "Born to Wander," an apt choice for a military dependent and future airman.

By the eleventh grade at Central High School in Omaha, Ramsey had bought a 442 "four on the floor" Oldsmobile he drove us around town in, to house parties and the prom. Our playlist now blasted from an external 8-track player plugged into the cigarette lighter socket. In summertime we joined the cavalcade of cars similarly blaring tunes and circling the narrow roads around Carter Lake. We grooved to the "music with a message" songs of Philly International. We found an appreciation for the blues of B. B. King, Bobby "Blue" Bland, and Albert King. We branched out to jazz artists who included Herbie Hancock, Stanley Turrentine, and Billy Cobham.

There were late nights, after busing tables at the Hilton, when Barry White and the Stylistics would sing of broken hearts. We commiserated over breakups, eating soul food and CD-sized sweet potato pies at Roseboro's on Thirtieth Street. (Okay, we didn't know they were that size. Compact discs had not yet been invented.)

In the spring and summer, we'd run, not jog, around Fontenelle Park near my house, past the lagoon where old men with tackle boxes cast for the catch of the day. Then we sat on my front porch, sipped water, and listened to KOWH, the "Sound of Soul" on the radio. On one occasion the Commodores' "This Is Your Life" played and no one said a word as Lionel Richie sang about making life-changing choices.

Those songs resonated. All of us were about to leave for the military and a future that was a blank canvas. Richardson and Ramsey enlisted in the army. Montgomery and I signed up for the air force. In 1975 we left Omaha with the unofficial theme song of our graduating class on our minds: Earth, Wind & Fire's "That's the Way of the World."

Richardson, Ramsey, and Montgomery returned to Omaha after

four-year hitches. I retired after twenty-two years in San Antonio, the place where music first grabbed me and hasn't let go.

The melodies keep playing through weddings, births, second careers, and the passing of loved ones. "Music made you think of life," Ramsey said. "Right versus wrong, and good versus evil. It helped us navigate through the world."

Music United Airmen in the 1970s

Dorm life in the U.S. Air Force was like living in an arena-sized FM radio, where the dial scrambled endlessly through every station. When the music hit you, it felt like a gale-force wind blown from an invisible huffing beast. As you walked past each door in the hallway, every musical genre had its say.

My first exposure to the white noise came in the mid-1970s at Ramstein Air Base in Germany and ended in the early 1980s at Lackland Air Force Base. We were sons of the seventies from different cultures, billeted at a two-story, Korean War–era dorm. Our differences in music gave us a glimpse into the other sides of our dorm mates' lives. We had one thing in common—playing our tunes on high-priced stereo component sets wired to earth-shaking speakers.

We scrimped, saved, and put the electronics on layaway. Pioneer was my choice—everything from the turntable, SX-650 receiver, cassette player/recorder, and two CS-05 round, wood, end-table omnidirectional speakers. From the time we woke until we turned in for the night, music echoed through the halls. It was a chaotic wave of blistering sound.

Santana's guitar screamed under the sway of a "Black Magic Woman." Boz Scaggs drawled about the dirty "Lowdown." Earth, Wind & Fire harmonized about the need to "Getaway." Diana Ross wailed she didn't want a cure for her "Love Hangover." Eddie

Rabbitt crooned about loving a rainy night. Freddy Fender lamented, "Wasted days and wasted nights." Willie Nelson and Waylon Jennings implored mamas not to let their babies grow up to be cowboys. From time to time, strains of Bach and Beethoven could be heard. The true rarity was the fan of the sci-fi TV classic "Star Trek" who had episodes on vinyl. We'd shake our heads when we'd hear Montgomery "Scotty" Scott yell he was pushing the Starship Enterprise to its limits.

During those surreal times, we learned the music that divided us could unite us. I learned to appreciate Pink Floyd and Jethro Tull down the hall one late night. Rockers would sit with us and sip wine as we savored Stevie Wonder's "Songs in the Key of Life." The older guys would call us into their room to listen to sixties rock and jazz as wisps of incense drifted like early morning fog. They'd rifle through crates of albums until they found a masterpiece. Then, like a scientist handling combustible liquids, they'd gently lower the needle on the groove of a deep cut that lifted them to nirvana.

On weekends we played spades, cranking up the music of Parliament-Funkadelic, the Isley Brothers, Heatwave, and the O'Jays to ear-splitting decibels. That's probably the reason many of us now mumble, "Huh, what'd you say?"

The cross-pollination of music led to summits in the day room, where we learned insights into one another. We picked up on why baseball meant the world to guys from the valley who'd played the sport on dirt lots since they were small; it didn't require expensive equipment, just a love for the game.

Disciples of soul gave a head nod to captains of R&B/soft rock ambassadors, like Steely Dan, Michael McDonald, and Kenny Loggins. The music played on as a player told us of losing a girlfriend after stepping out on her one time too many. Hall and Oates's song "She's Gone" would have been an apt needle drop for the soul, heavy with regret.

The smell of cologne and grilled-cheese sandwiches, charred on hot plates, often wafted in the sound-blasted halls. During sweltering summers we sat on the fire escape, arms cooled by hanging them out on a metal railing, the cheapest ice-cold beers in our hands.

Sergeants spun war stories of decades-old experiences, leaving us a road map to use and steer clear of life's hazards. The only times the volume was dialed down was for visits by family members, room inspectors, and lady friends. It was the way we blew off steam. We carried out support jobs that included delivering supplies, repairing vehicles, and administrative duties.

Promotions added responsibilities, and relationships dialed the volume back. The duel of the stereos ended as the sun set on disco and the dawn of the urban cowboys. We transferred to new assignments and moved off base to apartments where the music stayed low within the rented space.

If walls could talk, the saying would apply to the last barracks at Lackland I called home. It no longer stands, torn down years ago—now the site of a playground. Sometimes, as I drive by, I still see the sound factory in my mind's eye. I wonder if a youngster atop a jungle gym ever hears something strange that stops them mid-scramble.

I'd tell them it's nothing to worry about. It's just a faint melody from days when music once blasted at high volume from that very spot.

Remembering San Antonio's Disco Nights

The remains of disco lie buried across San Antonio, beneath layers of drywall, brick, and mortar.

When I drive on certain streets, I see more than a strip mall, nail shop, or warehouse. I see spaces where every night was a bustling, hustling dance party in a long-ago era. I see a time more than forty years ago, when we stepped out wearing Nik-Nik polyester shirts, creased bell-bottoms, and four-inch platform shoes. Young women wore halter tops and skintight spandex pants and ankle-length dresses with hems that rippled like twirling tops as they whirled on the dance floor.

Young club-goers from all walks of life crowded in dimly lit entryways, where forest-scented cologne clashed with floral-fragranced perfume. Spinning mirror balls reflected thousands of lights that dotted dancers like technicolor laser beams. At some clubs, white mist, swirling from fog machines, rolled across dance floors as cigarette smoke spiraled to gray hazy clouds on ceilings.

Disc jockeys spun records that blared the hiss of cymbals, rumble of bass guitars, and screaming of synthesizers. Dancers mobbed the floor to tunes by Heatwave, Evelyn "Champagne" King, Chic, and the Bee Gees. When the deejay dropped the needle on Donna Summer's "Last Dance," we knew it was closing time.

Recently I worked with the city's Office of Historic Preservation on a story about their ScoutSA online mapping program, which documents the city's culture, history, and heritage. As it turns out, there aren't any markers identifying buildings where dancers discoed until their feet ached and fingertips stung from snapping their fingers all night.

Discos were a refuge from the woes of a world that seemed on the verge of the end of days. Newscasts of the era showed the Jonestown massacre, the Three-Mile Island disaster, and the eruption of Mount Saint Helens. At the disco, we left those headlines in the parking lot, along with all of society's ills.

At the height of the era, from 1978 to 1979, all things seemed to revolve around disco, which is short for the French word *discotheque*, a nightclub where records are played for dancing. Musicians from the early 1970s churned out hits laced with R&B, Euro pop, and funk grooves that fueled a cultural explosion and spawned Van McCoy's "The Hustle," the movie *Saturday Night Fever*, and scores of dance clubs around the nation.

In San Antonio, the nightspots stretched across all zip codes, from the area near the San Antonio International Airport, along Austin Highway, down Saint Mary's Street, and through downtown to stretches of the West Side and South Military Drive. There isn't a definitive number for how many discos were operating in San Antonio, but they ranged from extravagant venues to holes-in-the-wall. Some clubs were more notable than ones we frequented, such as Déjà Vu and Hallelujah Hollywood, where long lines stretched to Coachlight Street near San Pedro Avenue.

Dancers arrived by the carload at the Nutcracker, tucked in the corner of a strip mall near North Star Mall. Players on the prowl sent drinks to fine-dressed divas, hoping their gesture would result in an invitation to deliver well-rehearsed pickup lines.

There was the Aquarium disco in the Basse West Shopping Center, on West Avenue, where birthday celebrants received free shots of tequila. The birthday person was almost guaranteed to leave a bit tipsy because each time they tried to down a shot, the host held their arm and they had to take another drink.

On South Military Drive, the best nachos, piled high on a plate, were found at the Chelsea Street Pub, which played disco music, inside South Park Mall, down from Close Encounters.

One hot spot became the namesake of San Antonian Burgundy Woods, who is named after a popular disco where her parents, Rachel and Sergio Rodriguez, met and fell in love. The glitz and music flowed into the couple's only child. In a 2021 San Antonio Stories column, Woods recalled that when other kindergarten students sang nursery rhymes, she would burst out the Bee Gees song "Stayin' Alive." So it's no surprise that she studied music in college and works in the fashion design industry.

Romance was in full bloom at many other clubs. Airmen from Lackland and Kelly Air Force Bases frequented Daddy Warbucks, outside of the Valley Hi gate of the basic military training base. On Wednesdays the club hosted Ladies Night and discounted alcoholic drinks to female guests.

But it was a Sunday evening when a young lady, wearing a formal black dress with a ruffled collar, sat with her bare feet propped in a banquet chair. She didn't want to be there, but she'd been coaxed by a friend to go out. A dismissive look colored her face as she politely turned away every guy who asked her to dance.

Across the dance floor, two young airmen watched as each denied dancer retreated to a nearby wall. The airman nearest to the dance floor was intrigued as the scene played out. After watching several rejections, he drained his drink and said, "I'm going to ask her to dance."

"Don't do that, man," his friend said. "She'll shoot you down like the other ones."

"Well," the daring airman said, "I won't be the only one."

When the dance floor cleared, he made his move. "Would you like to dance?" he said to the woman.

"Sure," she said. "Let me put on my shoes."

He wasn't expecting her answer. Neither was his friend, who looked as stunned as he felt. What he didn't know was she'd been eyeing him too, waiting for him to ask for a dance.

They danced to A Taste of Honey's "Boogie Oogie Oogie." They stayed on the floor for another, now forgotten, dance tune. Then Earth, Wind & Fire's "Reasons" played, and as they slow danced, his friend looked on, still stunned. After thanking her for the dance, the airman returned to the table.

"What was that?" his friend said.

"I don't know," the airman said, shrugging his shoulders. "It'll probably never happen again."

But as it turned out it wasn't their last dance. Other meetings led to dates as a nationwide backlash against disco closed the clubs they frequented. A courtship bloomed before the film *Urban Cowboy* ushered in country-themed nightspots where dancers tapped, stepped, and shuffled feet to the "Cotton-Eye Joe."

Marriage and a daughter preceded the age of music videos that took over the airwaves. In the twenty-first century, the rise of social media, digital downloads, and pocket-sized cellphones welcomed three granddaughters.

Today, forty-six years after that first dance, my wife and I—the young lady in the black dress and the young airman—are still together, still reminiscing about the days of disco.

CARRYING THE TORCH

Big Shoes to Fill

In April 1960 Charles Williams was picketing Joske's café, a downtown lunch counter that would not serve Black customers. A police officer, not in uniform, stopped him. "Who do you work for, boy?" the officer asked, planning to call the employer to have Williams removed from the picket line. Williams was self-employed, as a barber.

"Mr. Williams," he replied, handing the officer a business card. "Call him anytime."

The officer ripped up the card.

"I felt that was a blessing for me," Williams said. "I had a leader say, 'God put you in a position that other folks can't do.' I still believe that."

As the nation celebrates Martin Luther King Jr. Day on Monday, San Antonio civil rights activists are looking toward the next generation of change-makers. San Antonio leaders see promise in three of the newest members of the city's MLK commission, which organizes the annual march—Ananda Tomas, Trent Breitung, and Valerie Reiffert.

Dwayne Robinson, chair of the commission, said the trio brings a fresh perspective to the sixteen-member board. Tomas is the founder and executive director of ACT 4 SA, a police reform organization. Breitung is the digital organizer for the Texas Organizing Project, which strives to increase the political power and representation of people of color. Reiffert is cofounder of Radical Registrars, one of the few voter registration organizations led by Black women.

The younger activists have big shoes to fill. San Antonians such as Williams, Mario Salas, and Aaronetta Pierce fought for desegregation. They worked to improve conditions on the East Side, a predominantly Black part of town. They made San Antonio's march on Martin Luther King Jr. Day one of the largest in the nation.

Williams once marched against segregation beside the Reverend Claude Black, civil rights leader Harry Burns, and NAACP members. Now he owns the site of the former Saint Joseph's AME Church on Montana Street on the East Side. He turned it into the Williams Historical Museum, which features historical items from the pre–civil rights era to the present.

Six decades after the police officer questioned Williams, Tomas is working to reform policing. She said 2020 provided the perfect storm for unjust acts across the nation. In May of that year she joined thousands at Travis Park to protest the killing of George Floyd by Minneapolis police officers.

She believes fighting for change honors her ancestors and said that truly living King's dream means battling injustice. That's part of her duty to future generations. "We need folks fighting for change. I hope we focus on moving forward and the people who are pushing that envelope even more."

Salas, a member of the county's historical commission who has taught African American studies, joined the Floyd protests to support Tomas and her generation's call to arms. "I'm proud of her and the group that doesn't give up," Salas said. "To this day, when you see it, you love it."

Salas was ten when he was walking to a movie downtown and was intrigued by the sight of Williams and other protesters at Joske's. He asked a woman in line if he could carry a picket sign and join the protest. She told him no, that he needed to ask his mother. Salas returned another day, picked up a sign, and joined his first protest anyway.

Several years later, as a member of the Student Nonviolent Coordinating Committee, he marched against discrimination and the death of Bobby Joe Phillips, a San Antonio Black man beaten by police. Williams is delighted when he sees a young person step up. He admires young folks who are daring and making a difference.

Last week at the museum Williams talked with Salas about the days when he was one of the young protesters Williams called "rabble-rousers."

"I recall a gentleman saying to me one time, 'A washing machine is no good without an agitator,'" he said. "And that's what they are—they're agitators; they keep things going."

Salas said that's what the late U.S. Rep. John Lewis, D-Georgia, called for—"good trouble."

"Before it gets better, we'll have to go through some rough times," Williams predicted. "After each storm, there's a rainbow. I do believe that we will see a beautiful rainbow for this country. At the end of the day, right wins out."

Pierce agreed. She grew up in Nashville, Tennessee, during the Jim Crow era, not far from historically Black universities and colleges. Striving for excellence against all odds was the baton her ancestors handed down. She became well versed in African American history, an advocate of youth, and respected across the city, qualities that prompted then mayor Henry Cisneros to select her as inaugural chair of the MLK commission.

Pierce said one of the challenges today's torchbearers face are entities that want to rule others' bodies and orientations. "A democracy of the people, by the people, for the people is exactly that," she said. "We need to learn to stay out of the lanes that infringe on the rights of other people."

Becoming a mother prompted Reiffert to take action in the city where she was born and raised. She said she came out of her fog after seeing the killings of Trayvon Martin and other Black men across the nation. "It feels like it's something that had to be done. I feel grateful to be in a position to effect change."

Breitung is encouraged by young activists, such as the march's scheduled guest speakers, fighting for economic and environmental justice. This year's speakers are Anya Dillard, a community activist and social entrepreneur; Jerome Foster II, the youngest member of the White House Environmental Justice Advisory Council in the Biden administration; and Amariyanna Copeny, a sixteen-year-old who says she is a future president.

"There's a lot at stake," Breitung said. "The civil rights leaders, they fought for a lot. Maybe we haven't seen the progress they envisioned years ago. We feel like we need to win it, so the pressure is there, but what an honor."

Safe Spaces Listed in Green Book

There were few places for Black travelers to rest their heads at night in the Jim Crow era. The Ritz Motel on the city's East Side offered refuge. Opened in 1953, it was one of San Antonio's first Black motels.

Pinkie Smith—a prominent San Antonio businessman in the mid-1900s—owned the one-story, twenty-four-room hotel at 2958 East Commerce Street. Shirley Allen, eighty-one, was familiar with the safe space. She and her husband, Dr. Paul Allen, stayed in room no. 1 when they traveled to San Antonio from Marshall in 1963.

The motel was listed in their *Negro Motorist Green Book*—a publication Allen never traveled without. During segregation, Black motorists weren't welcome at most white restaurants and motels across the nation. The travel annual mapped locales where Black motorists could stay without fear of harassment or discrimination.

Today the motel is one of eleven *Green Book* sites highlighted in recent Black history research by the San Antonio African American Community Archive and Museum, with help from the city and Pamela Walker, assistant professor of history at Texas A&M University–San Antonio.

"Much of what I talk about is preserving the history because there is so much erasure," said Walker, whose students did much of the research. "All of my students are from San Antonio, born and raised here, and have never heard this history before. It's really important that we bring the community in, young people and longtime community members. That's the only way that we will preserve it."

Walker and her students helped assemble a map of the spots listed and invited the community to travel with them to put markers at each site. The initiative is part of the city's three-year effort to preserve African American heritage through grants from the Texas Historical Commission, National Park Service, and San Antonio Conservation Society.

Allen brought her original 1963–64 *Green Book*, sealed in a plastic zip-close bag. "For Vacation without Aggravation," read the tagline on the emerald cover. Sixty years after she stayed at the motel with her late husband, the site is an empty lot off of Commerce Street across from the Claude W. Black Community Center. There were complaints that the building was rundown in the 1980s, and it was turned into an education center. Years later it was demolished—the fate of several landmarks on the *Green Book* list. Allen was shocked that the Ritz Motel no longer existed but happy the museum and its partners offered a glimpse of a time when a travel guide helped Black travelers avoid harassment, physical harm, and danger.

"It was like a dream that this has happened," she said.

Inside her $1.95 travel guide was another tie to that era—a folded newspaper article in pristine shape except for the yellowing of time. An Associated Press story from 1963 was attached to the back cover with a paper clip. The headline reads "Texas Cities Act to Desegregate."

In San Antonio, a city council committee set July 4 as the target date for the voluntary desegregation of privately owned businesses. At the time 216 restaurants and 33 motels had pledged to open their doors to all races. Allen had marked the first integrated eatery where they would dine—a Luby's cafeteria at 4922 Broadway.

"Don't ever get rid of that book," Allen recalled her late husband saying. "Now, I know why."

After passengers boarded the bus at Tony G's Soul Food restaurant, it rolled past a stop sign beneath an Interstate 37 overpass where the Monte Carlo Cave Club once stood. Tom and Julia Smith owned the club and welcomed patrons of all races. The couple also owned Smith's Cafe, where residents and travelers could enjoy fine cuisine.

The tour continued past the Zumbro Center once located at 621 East Commerce. Across the street from Sunset Station, the three-story building held a hotel, barber shop, and offices. Three of Walker's students spoke about each of the tour sites.

Krista Guajardo, thirty-one, told passengers about Hicks Beauty School and the Three Point Beauty Parlor. James Thomas, forty-one, talked about Carter-Taylor Mortuary, and Vanessa Godsey, thirty-seven, spoke about Smith's Cafe and the Ritz Motel.

New buildings are being built at 126 North Cherry Street, once home to the Mason Hotel, where the sounds of jazz filled the halls and guests dined on soul food on Sundays. The hotel, owned by Rachel Mason, served as a business hub and community meeting place. The business closed in the early 1970s. In 2008 bulldozers demolished the structure. Student researchers said the hotel was razed before the San Antonio Conservation Society could verify its historical integrity and whether the site should be preserved.

A paved lot at 328 South Pine Street was the home of Hicks Beauty School. Owned by Jessie Mae Hicks, the school offered day and night classes to young women and free services to those in need. The school had a dormitory, cafeteria, and laundry area. Hicks offered grants, scholarships, and accepted GI Bill grants. It burned down in 1994.

"It was so monumental at the time, and it doesn't even exist anymore," Guajardo said.

Houses span the space at 716 Virginia Boulevard, where Jane Pink Brown's Three-Point Beauty Parlor opened in February 1946. Brown rented a room for extra income at the parlor where East Side residents gathered to socialize. The parlor, which had a barbershop and air conditioning, burned down in 1973.

The Carter-Taylor-Williams Mortuary at 601 Center Street was the only structure on the tour still standing. During segregation Black funeral homeowners were community leaders, and travel guides provided mortuary addresses to travelers who might need aid during a visit to a foreign town. Thomas's research revealed how one of the owners, James E. Taylor, an NAACP chairman, planned a memorial march for slain civil rights leader and NAACP field secretary Medgar Evers, killed in 1963 by a white supremacist in Mississippi.

"It's important that it gets out there," Thomas said. "This is history that's happened right here in San Antonio that a majority of people, inside and outside of the Black community, didn't know about."

Victor Hugo Green created the *Negro Motorist Green Book*, which listed diverse businesses nationwide that were safe for Black motorists. Green, a Black postman from Harlem, published the guide after he and his wife, Alma, faced discrimination at stops on a car trip. His first fifteen-page travel guide highlighted businesses in metropolitan New York that welcomed African Americans. It's believed he modeled his annual after the Jewish Vacation Guide, which offered safe places where Jews could stop while traveling. In the 1948 issue Green wrote of a day in the future "when the guide would not have to be published."

"That is when we as a race will have equal opportunities and privileges in the United States," he wrote. "It will be a great day for us to suspend this publication for then we can go wherever we please, and without embarrassment."

Green never lived to see that day. He died on October 16, 1960. Passage of the Civil Rights Act of 1964 banned segregation in public places, reducing the need for the book. It ceased publication in 1967.

Deborah Omowale Jarmon, SAAACAM's CEO and director, recalled two things her father carried on their trips to visit family from Columbus, Ohio, to Selma, Alabama: a *Green Book* and AAA trip guide. She said people at stores and gas stations where they stopped knew her father by name. The stops were safe spaces like those in San Antonio listed in the annual.

The guides and Walker staked signs at each stop that read, "There's a Story Here." Passersby can stop and scan a QR code with their cellphone for the full story of the site. Jarmon said they plan to share other locations on the West Side.

"These spaces shine a light and provide a reflection on a time that perhaps people don't want to remember," Jarmon said. "This is a reminder of Black resistance, resilience, progress, and Black joy."

BARBERSHOP CLIPS

Barbershop Talk Recalls a Fading East Side

The scenery along East Commerce Street includes two men sitting in the shade outside Taylor's Barber Shop. Most motorists pass without a glance, but those who know the pair honk, wave, and shout from car windows. The men respond in kind before surveying the next round of passersby from their sidewalk perch.

On a typical day, Prince "Smiley" Simms leans back in a low, orange, vinyl folding chair, an ivy cap slung low over his forehead. Paul White sits across from him on a high four-legged stool beside an open door spilling the sounds of 1970s soul singers and bluesmen howling about cheating love and hard times. Both men are barbers. White, eighty-five, is the owner. Simms, fifty-eight, is his partner. They're keepers of traditions that have played out in men's lives from cradle to casket. When business lags, this is where you can find them, on the busy East Side street watching life roll by.

Years ago they didn't have time to sit outside. They were too busy cutting hair and listening to stories—about families, race, sports, politics, everything. In its heyday, from the 1940s through the early 1950s, White's place was the main Black barbershop on the East Side.

Fathers and sons sought out the seven barbers, five men and two women, for haircuts that cost seventy-five cents. Now customers pay twelve dollars for a trim. It was a place where parents brought their boys for knowledge they couldn't glean from textbooks. It was a place steeped in history, culture, and the ways to become a man, a place where White and his barbers had the authority to correct any child who got out of line (and they had the approval of the parents). Usually all it took was one look.

"I tell young men to keep their head on if they want to get ahead," White says. "But youngsters of today, you can't talk to them. Parents would drop them off with me, and I'd tear their behinds up if they acted up. I can't discipline them now. They tell me, 'You're old school.'"

Over the years White's barbers left, taking a share of customers and opening their own shops that met the demands of changing times. But White still maintains a loyal following. Many customers drive from all points for personalized service, a dash of old-school tonic, and spirited talk. The customers range from boys to older men. The majority are Black, but Latino and Anglo customers stop in too. Neighborhood regulars, military retirees, San Antonio transplants, former San Antonio Spurs, and tourists in need of a touch-up have all patronized Taylor's.

Simms sparks sports talk and daily pokes at White's favorite team, the Spurs. He promotes the accomplishments of neighborhood youngsters by plastering newspaper clippings of their football and basketball team wins beside collegiate and pro write-ups.

Marvin King Sr. arrived for his monthly haircut as Regina Belle sang about good things coming to those who wait. "No fade in the back," King says to White, patting the nape of his neck. "And I need it off the sides. How are your grandkids doing?"

King says he has only let one other barber cut his hair in the past twenty-five years, and he never went back. The man talked too much to pay attention to what he was doing. "It's a testament to his tenacity as a person and quality of work that people still come here," says King, who drives in from the North Side. "I come here just for the barbershop; it's a special trip and it's worth it."

Retired army colonel Reginald J. Sapenter, eighty, walks in and hangs his baseball cap, stitched with "Purple Heart" and gold clusters across the bill, on a hat rack. He gets a "You're next" from White.

While White clips Sapenter's gray hair, the Reverend Hector J. Grant Sr. talks about his calling, reminiscing about preachers carpooling through the South in the 1960s and a pastor who worked part-time as a ranch hand in West Texas who didn't break horses but gentled them. "This is a repository of stories," says Grant, sixty-three. "It's one of the fine institutions that are now dying."

White recalls when the community and East Commerce Street bustled with Black businesses, and soldiers and patrons packed the sidewalks. Now he looks out at buildings lining the street and remembers what they were decades ago. He rubs his jaw with his thumb, watching several men cart wood and supplies into an old building across the street. "That used to be a Texaco station," he says, pointing. "Now it's going to be some kind of convenience store."

White points across the street to Hernandez Tire Shop, once a nightclub that closed as he was opening the shop at 8 a.m. Bellinger's Taxi Stand, the only cab service for Blacks, was located where a corrugated garage now sits beside the tire shop. A dry-cleaning store was once a full-service Gulf gas station. And a vacant lot to the south on the next block was where the Lifesaver Café was located. Patrons ate there twenty-four hours a day, White says, and it was known for the best enchiladas around. North of the shop was the only white restaurant on the street. For many years Blacks could get food to go but not sit down for a meal. White walked a picket line outside of the eatery to protest the policy. After days of picketing, the owners closed the restaurant.

Then the government built Interstate 37. Land was bought and homes bulldozed near the barbershop's original location on Chestnut Street. The highway, White says, led to faraway air-conditioned malls and ranch-style homes on the North Side, where Blacks worked but never lived. "Integration helped in one way," he says of changes in his neighborhood. "And it killed it in another way."

White has clipped hair at the same shop for sixty-two years. He took up the scissors and clippers after a stint in the army from 1944 to 1946. A black-and-white picture below his barber's license shows him wearing a wide-lapel suit around the time the shop's original owner, Verley Taylor, hired him in 1946. He learned early to listen to customers and concentrate on cutting with a steady hand.

White prides himself on remembering a customer's preference after one look. "The only time I shake is if I get angry," White says. "I used to get angry, but I don't do that anymore."

Photos of his family line the counter. His grandchildren share space on the counter behind him with a copy of *Jet* magazine. In a black-and-white wallet-size photo, White stands beside his wife of fifty-eight years, Geraldine, who died four years ago.

Directly above him hangs a framed portrait of his son, Paul N. White, a manager for Southwestern Bell who called him every Friday night. He died of a heart attack, and White proudly displays a resolution from the city honoring his son's service to the community.

These days the shop is the anchor in his life. He says he'll keep cutting hair as long as his hands are steady. "I don't have no deadline. I can't sit at home and do nothing."

So he makes his way to the shop, to the sound of buzzing clippers and customers and Simms's daily jabs at his Spurs. When their customers thin out, the barbers sit outside on their turf talking to neighbors and strangers passing by. The occupants of the glory days are gone. The landscape is changing with the push of downtown expansion. Any hint of the hustling and bustling era is gone, except for the pair still simmering with old community pride.

Barber Hangs up His Clippers after Seventy Years

Bobby Johnson's mother and grandmother brought him to Andy's Barber Shop for his first haircut at one year old; the year was 1954. Nearly seventy years later Johnson calls Andy Banda, the only barber he's ever known, Tío. "He's family to me," Johnson, sixty-seven, said.

One recent drizzly day Johnson drove Banda, ninety-six, to the shop in the Alamo Hardwoods building at 904 West Laurel in the old Five Points neighborhood north of downtown. Banda inched his walker across the wet sidewalk, and Johnson helped him inside. After seventy years the nonagenarian is turning off his clippers and closing his business because of illness.

Following the pair, photojournalist Jerry Lara and I looked up to see model airplanes hanging from the ceiling, forming a constellation of warbirds from the past. Two barber chairs were bolted to a green and white checkered tile floor, but it was the box of magazines that swept me back to my childhood.

My great-grandfather—Theodore H. Martin, a World War II army veteran—often took me for haircuts in Columbus, Georgia. As he and fellow veterans, church deacons, and brickyard working men solved the ills of the world, I'd flip through periodicals like *Argosy*, *Ebony*, and *Popular Mechanics* fanned out on a table like a gambler's hand of cards. When retired *San Antonio Express-News* reporter John

MacCormack asked if I was interested in a story about the barber and customers' long relationship, he had me at "barber."

Entering Banda's shop is like walking back in time. Photos of buildings and businesses long gone dot the green-striped walls. A can of Barbasol shaving cream, a bottle of Lucky Tiger aftershave, and a tin of white talc line the counters. A sign reading "Proud to be a Mason" shares wall space with certificates, a caricature of Banda, and newspaper clippings. A sepia-toned photo of a younger Banda, in suit and tie, is wedged in the corner of his framed Texas barber license.

Being in the shop reminded me of the cast of regulars found at barbershops in all zip codes: contrary cusses, diplomats, skeptics, and the watcher who never says a word. His customers have included workaday men, former police chief Fred Palmer, and former mayor Sam Bell Steves.

Banda flipped a switch, and the barbershop pole outside lit up with red, white, and blue stripes swirling top to bottom. He told tales of loyal customers who frequented his shop and was thankful to the building owners for providing him with "seventy years of shelter."

He was born Andres H. Banda on November 30, 1924, to Tony and Luz Banda in Victoria. Growing up, his father had one hairstyle for him—a soldier's cut—shaved to the scalp. Banda decided he wanted to cut hair professionally after seeing his barber, Juan Guerra, dressed in a clean, white long-sleeved shirt, garters on the arms, and a tie.

"That's what impressed me to become a barber," Banda said.

Another incentive was not working in the sun and sweltering heat, like his father, a carpenter. During World War II Banda served three and a half years in the Army Air Corps, stationed in Hawaii and Japan. After the war he returned home to Victoria, where the segregation he left was still in place. He moved to San Antonio and, in June 1946, attended the former Lewis Barber College near San Fernando Cathedral. After six months of training, he apprenticed with a master barber for three years. With $750 in savings, he opened the barbershop in November 1951. Harry Truman was president. Winston Churchill was the United Kingdom's prime minister.

Banda's first customer was a bus driver—one of the steady stream of customers from the San Antonio Transit Company across the street. He said in the early 1970s he set a personal record—cutting fifty-two customers' hair from 7 a.m. to 9:30 p.m. on a Christmas Eve.

These days the barber sees many old cronies, not in person but in photos printed in the newspaper's obituary section.

Speaking of the departed, he reminisced about Hortense, his late wife of fifty-three years. "She was beautiful," he said. "She gave me two daughters and a son."

For the past thirty-three years Johnson has been known as KSYM deejay Bobby J, with a vinyl jazz show on Saturday mornings at San Antonio 90.1 FM. On air, from the San Antonio College campus, he plays tunes from the golden age of jazz with a heaping of behind-the-scene stories.

Blocks from the broadcast booth he sat still for Banda, just as he learned the first time he sat on a children's board propped in the barber's chair. Banda draped a blue pin-striped cape around Johnson, covering him from his neck to his knees. As the barber cut away stray hairs with his buzzing clippers and combed waves into place, Johnson recalled how styles evolved from flattops to long hair over the years and prices rose from the original fee of thirty-five cents to fifteen dollars and more.

"Okay, Bobby," Banda said as he finished the job. He put away his tools near combs and razors submerged in a jar of blue Barbicide. In the shop's heyday, it was the source of a strong antiseptic smell that's now faded.

"Thank you, Andy," Johnson replied, and handed twenty dollars to Banda. The barber held his palms up as if to say "We're good." Johnson nodded and tucked the bill away.

The faithful patron, who regularly checks on the veteran hair cutter's welfare, grabbed a red broom and swept hair clippings into a dustpan. Before Banda locked the door, Johnson slipped five dollars into his shirt pocket.

That day Johnson, one of the true regulars at the Five Points shop, received what he'd hoped for years ago—Banda the barber's last haircut.

This Shop Will Buzz No More

The men pulled up in trucks made in America. They drove in from La Vernia, China Grove, and New Berlin. Some came from Marion, New Braunfels, and Devine, rural places forged when Texas was an open frontier. They wore scuffed cowboy boots and faded jeans for function not fashion. They spoke the same language, spinning conversations about show horses and livestock. They lamented the loss of a five dollar haircut, and tall tales that grew like biscuits on an old cast-iron stove. It's the last roundup for the Collins Barber Shop.

Mike Collins, owner of the East Side stop, is closing his shop at W. W. White Road and Shelburn Street after forty-nine years. Collins, seventy-three, chose to shut down after his partner Howard Lynn fell ill recently. The news sparked a long trail of regulars to the shop since he announced that today would be his last day of business.

Freddie Biesenbach, seventy-five, stood in front of the wall mirror Wednesday morning, raking a comb through his just-trimmed hair. Larry Burns, sixty-four, and Robert Halbardier, seventy-one, sat in leather chairs under a painting of white stallions galloping at full tilt. The trio kept the talk flowing. "I came here from Bulverde," Biesenbach said, dangling a toothpick from the corner of his mouth like a fishing pole. "This is better than going to a therapist."

Burns sat in the barber chair for his time under the clippers. "Now I'll have to go to the beauty shop," he said, laughing as Collins snipped his hair. "This place is an institution. I don't know where I'm going to get a haircut."

Burns's fellow customers shared his quandary. They frequented the shop from 6 a.m. to noon through the week for decades. They're farmers, ranchers, and cowhands who gathered for more than grooming and a splash of Lucky Tiger hair tonic. It was about keeping the ways of a simpler life alive.

Collins's uncle, Roy Lee "Unk" Collins, opened the four-chair shop in 1959 and barbered until his death in 1971. Collins and Lynn, both part-timers at the time, have worked full-time ever since. Much has passed by over the years. Nearby fields and pastures, once bare, are covered with fast food stops, stores, and gas stations. But the talk never changed. Conversations kick off with "howdy," barreling into talks about horse racing, rain, weather, family, and the old-timers long gone.

They were men like the customer who saddled his palomino and rode the horse to his shop, tying it to a post like riders in the Old West. Those were the days when Sydney Powell brought her son in and watched him scoot onto a vinyl-covered board resting on the armrests. That was his routine until he turned ten years old and wanted a high-class cut.

"They go to unisex shops for a state-of-the-art haircut, but it's not the same," Powell, fifty-seven, said. "He doesn't appreciate what he lost. One day he'll look back and say those haircuts I got from Mike were the best."

Collins only cuts one woman's hair. Yolanda Olivarri, a longtime friend, trusts only Collins to trim her waist-long hair. She showed up for her final cut on Wednesday morning, standing beside his chair as he clipped split ends away. She's helped him at the shop for a dozen years, stopping in from time to time to help sweep up hair clippings.

"This is their life," she said, watching the three men wave and leave a place where honor was more than a catchphrase. The graying barber isn't one to get emotional, even when customers whipped up nostalgic yarns. But he's on the same page with his customers on one thing—this is the last hurrah.

The mornings of putting on his white smock, gray jeans, and pumpkin-colored cowboy boots are at an end. Collins's furnishings are stuffed in moving boxes sitting under a mounted jackalope, the crossbreed critter of Texas lore. This afternoon the shop will be dusty memories, carried away by a passel of rugged men, doting mothers, and one longhaired woman.

"I'll miss the store," Collins said, standing beside the last barber chair. "Some of these stories are true, and some of them ought to be true."

San Antonio Barber's Shop on Wheels

The summer heat felt like a blast from a furnace when Julio Garanzuay, thirty-nine, brought his sons Ramiro Villy, twelve, and Julio Garanzuay, eight, for haircuts from Christopher "Chris DaBarber" Flores. Inside Flores's Big Shots Barber Lounge, it was chilly.

The forty-six-year-old barber, wearing a dark blue New York Yankees baseball cap, welcomed the trio. He clicked on his silent clippers to first trim Ramiro's shock of hair as his brother tapped away at a game on a cellphone.

"They call me little Julio. He's big Julio," the youngster said, with a nod to his father.

The older Garanzuay gazed around the barbershop on wheels. The fourteen-by-seven-foot trailer was parked at a lot at Potranco Road and Loop 1604. It has a silver diamond-plated sheet metal floor. A flat-screen TV, connected to Wi-Fi, anchored a corner near the door. Jars of Johnny B. Mode styling gel and Pacinos styling paste rested on bookshelves. A portable air conditioner, powered by a mini-split, two-ton generator, cooled the white-walled space. Bolted outside is the barbers' calling card—a red, white, and blue striped barber pole.

"It's a clean setup," Garanzuay said. "It's pretty impressive. It's more personal, one on one, no distractions and more access to more clients."

Flores's lounge is a reflection of the coronavirus-changing times. It's one of several mobile salons offering haircuts on the go across San Antonio. Flores cuts his customers' hair six days a week at parking lots on the Northwest Side, posting spots where he'll be on social media, including Instagram and Facebook.

Longtime and new clients flock to his black mobile grooming trailer, pulled by a white Dodge Ram truck. Before the pandemic Flores had a fixed location near the South Texas Medical Center, with a robust roster of clients. Offering haircuts on the move became an option when the virus brought business to a halt.

In January he started thinking about food trucks around him and wondered if he could customize a shop on wheels. Flores said he consulted with the Fud Trailer Company. He wanted a trailer gutted of inside appliances and built to his design. He saved up for the first payment of the double-axle trailer, which can run between $13,000 and $18,000. The only remnant of a food truck on the custom trailer was a service window. A friend mounted a 12,000-watt generator that powers the unit.

On May 19 Flores picked up the trailer. After thirty days of preparation and paperwork, he rolled his grooming station onto the road. "I wanted to create something different," he said. "More of a come-to-you service."

Flores became interested in the art of grooming as a little boy when his grandfather took him to a barbershop in Nacogdoches. He was captivated by the barber, Mr. Arriola. The man, in his sixties, wore sharp, ironed clothes. He used clippers attached to a clear plastic hose that vacuumed up shorn hair. But the most impressive thing about the barber was his two-tone 5.0 Mustang, a gray-bottom, blue-topped clean machine parked outside.

Flores learned to listen without prejudice, not interrupt, and store information away for future access. Arriola let Flores use his first clippers to touch up the hair of the regulars. His lessons took place under the unblinking glass eyes of a deer's head mounted on a wall. The two-chair shop's carpet captured the scent of blue hair tonic and white talc from the barbers.

Ten years ago Flores moved to San Antonio and worked at Ray's Barber Shop on the West Side. He said Ray Gonzalez taught him about life and how to use money to make money. Flores shares those lessons on his YouTube channel, "Big Shots Barber Lounge."

"I'm letting other barbers know this is the future," he said. "I want to show there are plenty of opportunities out here. Saving time and gas is a real convenience for customers these days."

After Flores finished Ramiro's hair, Garanzuay motioned for little Julio to climb into the chair. The youngster grimaced as the barber fastened the cape around his neck. As he finished, Julio was ready to get out of the chair.

"You want some gel in your hair?" Flores asked the youngster.

"No, I'm fine," Julio said.

His father said, "You need some gel."

"Yeah," Flores added, "let's see how it looks with some product."

The barber combed blue gel into the boy's hair. He leaned back like an artist eyeing a painting and inspected the smooth locks laid to the right, above shaved sides.

"Whoooo!" Flores said. "That's fresh!"

Julio looked in the mirror and gave his approval.

As 5 p.m. stop-and-go traffic packed lanes on 1604, Abel Orta, forty-two, walked in with his son Matthew, sixteen. The teen wanted a taper fade cut. The Ortas have followed Flores for a few years, happy with his style of grooming. "I love to see him get better and prosperous in the business," Orta said. "He's a go-getter."

Driving to get styled by Flores is not a problem for the father and son. "He's been my guy," Matthew said. "I cannot go anywhere else."

THOSE WITHOUT A VOICE

Only Texas Is Big Enough for This Pet

In Marin Hollow, deep in the Helotes Hill Country, lives a pet unlike the cats and dogs in the area. He's Red the longhorn, a mischievous steer that's the color of rusty leaves. His horns stretch more than six feet tip to tip and slope like an old cowhand's handlebar mustache. He weighs more than six hundred pounds and is thick as an oil barrel.

"He's not fat. He's just big-boned," said Denise Moore, a neighbor he's followed since he was a calf. "He's a funny guy."

Red spends most of his day at Moore's property, named Rachmones, which means compassion in Yiddish. Her husband, Craig Manifold, and their three children—Hanna, twenty-three; Della, twenty; and Caleb, eleven—all have stories of adventures with Red among the scrub brush and mesquite tree-lined fields. He's photobombed an outside father-and-son portrait. He's lapped up water from their swimming pool. And when it's time to go home he's liable to gallop around Moore's house, with his owner, Pat Langlinais, in hot pursuit.

Born in Boerne, Red was purchased by Langlinais six years ago as a hobby. He hand-fed the calf that's grown almost as tall as a compact car. Red, the only longhorn on his property, was raised around horses on Moore's adjacent land. "He's just an oversized dog with horns," said Langlinais, forty-nine. "He likes to lick your hand; he's pretty gentle."

In recent years cattle have become a roadside attraction for travelers across the state. And increasingly more people have taken them in as pets. According to the Presidential Pet Museum, President George W. Bush kept a longhorn named Ofelia at his ranch in Crawford.

Longhorns like Red have been called yard art or pasture ornaments, but some breeders and ranchers take offense at use of the terms. They stress that longhorns are livestock, noted for their ability to adapt to harsh conditions and their lean cuts of beef.

Laura Standley, editor of *Texas Longhorn Trails Magazine*, said that people raise the animals for many reasons, such as an agricultural tax exemption. "It's different things to different people. They are all unique, sizes, patterns, and horn sizes; they're not just a standard cow. No two are the same."

The editor added that some people keep the animals for nostalgia, with a nod to descendants who once drove cattle herds. "It's that historical remembrance of yesteryear," she said, "and the romanticism of the cowboys."

Langlinais said Red spends most of his time with Moore and her family. He's also bonded with their dogs, Dexter and Cash, both tripods, and Teddy and Duckie. There's also Ty and Kona, two fosters from Spay Neuter Inject Protect of San Antonio.

Moore, a homeschool teacher, said this longhorn appreciates the written word. While she was reading to her son in their barn, Red hung his head over a chain, watching them, lost in the tale of Mary Shelley's *Frankenstein*. In the near future many more people may be aware of Red's exploits. Moore said she has a children's book about the friendly steer in the making. There's apt to be a page in the book about Red's aversion to being fenced in.

He's twisted his horns side to side to get through a walk-in garage door. And he's jumped a five-foot fence and slipped beneath chains just to be near his clan. "Feed him the good stuff, feed him first, and you won't have any problems," she said. "And the only way to get him to go is if he wants to go."

Missions Have Faith in Their Cats

They're the pros, exterminating vermin that creep past the perimeter of Mission Espada on the South Side. Cloaked in stealth and silence, they corner mice, snatch snakes from kitchen cupboards, and bat away scorpions. They aren't bonded or insured, but their skill for stalking prey speaks for itself. The protectors of the eighteenth-century mission are two large cats—Dominic and Moses—and they're on a mission from God to keep the holy space free of pests.

They're the pets of Brother Jerome Wolnik, sixty-five, a Franciscan missionary and gardener who tends to the plush greenery and flowers that bloom around the grounds not far from the San Antonio River. When he drives through the gates from Mission San José, where he lives, the mousers report for duty. "These guys take care of everything," he said. "Moses has the red collar. Dominic has the blue, and he says the rosary every day."

Wolnik's order was founded by Saint Francis of Assisi, the patron saint of animals and the environment, so it's natural for the cats to coexist peacefully with the church. In recent months the mousers have been busy. Wolnik said heavy machinery clearing land around the San Antonio River as part of the $245.7 million Mission Reach restoration project has driven snakes, scorpions, rats, and lizards from the riverbanks toward the mission looking for shelter.

There was a time centuries ago when cats were linked to witchcraft and paganism, beliefs that almost led to their extinction. But over time parishes began taking them into cathedrals and churches to control rodents. Wolnik joked that care for the cats, including vaccinations and sterilizations, is budgeted under rodent control. He said the two are healthy and hearty because they do their job so well.

When he drives through the gate at 5:30 a.m., they jump on the hood of his pickup, leaving a trail of paw prints and meowing to be fed. Wolnik has had cats at the mission since 1995, when he found a snake coiled in a kitchen corner. "I said, 'No way.' That's it, I got a cat."

He's had Dominic since he was born in the pantry thirteen years ago. He named the white, black-spotted cat after the Dominican Order, whose followers wear black hoods and white habits.

Three years ago, on the wheel well of a pickup at a Walgreens parking lot, he found Moses—a little white and orange fuzzball barely the size of a blackboard eraser. It was August 6, the day of the Feast of the Transfiguration that celebrates when Moses and Elijah appeared with Jesus on Mount Tabor.

"It was either Elijah or Moses, and the vet couldn't spell Elijah," Wolnik said of naming Dominic's apprentice. "So we named him Moses."

Leslie Price, business manager of the mission, said Wolnik babies his cats like a proud parent. "He's one of a kind. They know who their daddy is." She said the friary is like a household where everyone shares everything, including feeding the cats. Several other cats have tried to make the mission their home, but the lead mouser didn't accept them.

"Dominic takes one look [at them] and says, 'There's the river. You can do your own fishing, and it's better for you to stay on the other side,'" Wolnik said.

So far, Moses is the only cat Dominic has tutored in his catechism.

Wolnik said the cats have become an attraction at the mission, spawning their own fan base. Tourists snap pictures of the pair as much as they do the rustic property.

When children approach the pair, Wolnik said Moses will roll on his back for a belly rub, as if to say, "Here I am, Lord. I come to do your will."

Wolnik said Dominic is the opposite; rubs aren't his thing. Saint Francis medals dangle from the collars of both cats, which are as big as raccoons. They're outdoor cats and only come inside on the coldest nights. When it rains they seek cover under the arches of the iconic mission bell tower. "They like the perching element," he said.

Cats aren't unique to just Mission Espada. Nine cats call Mission San Juan home. Since he arrived fourteen years ago, Father Jim Galvin, pastor of Mission San Juan, has had cats to control rodents. He has three inside felines—Chico, fourteen; Cappuccino, seven; and eighteen-month-old Lily, whom he found abandoned while making a sick call—and six outside cats that appear like a flash mob whenever he opens a bag of food.

He's closest to Chico, who trails him like a dog when he strolls through the woods near the riverbanks. Sometimes at dusk, while walking and reflecting, he'll hear wild pigs rustle in the brush. And in a rare moment an armadillo will waddle into view. "For me, God is everywhere," Galvin said. "One of the nicest places is in the evening, surrounded by nature, and the cat jumps and runs among the flies."

Father David Garcia, director of the Old Spanish Missions, is familiar with the cats of the missions. He said it makes sense that cats are part of the missions, not only to protect but also to add to the tranquility.

"We've tried to make the missions sacred places of prayer and reflection. The relationship [Galvin and Wolnik] have with the cats is a part of their peacefulness; the cats help them to connect them to nature. I kind of feel the cats provide a sense of serenity."

Animal Care Services spokeswoman Lisa Norwood said the missions are setting an example for the community. “The visitors probably have a more enjoyable experience without the vermin that would probably be there if the cats weren’t there,” she said. “They’re stepping up, allowing these cats to be cats and providing them with a loving home.”

It's No Kind of Dog's Life on City Streets

Responding to a call from a Good Samaritan one cool morning, Animal Care Services officer Gabe Rodriguez spotted the black-and-white dog that had been reported roaming near Camargo Park on the Southwest Side. Once the dog was secured, however, she kept tugging at the leash, trying to lead Rodriguez up an easement near woods where javelinas rustled in the brush.

The determined dog took Rodriguez and other officers through high weeds and clinging burrs to a five-foot-high mound made of flood debris and timber washed up from Leon Creek.

Yelps echoed through the woods. The officers, after digging through a patch of dry grass, found out why the dog had dragged them up the pasture. Her three pups were hidden in a hollowed-out den.

"She was a true stray dog that started getting domesticated," ACS officer Joseph Flores said, "because people started to feed her."

Thousands of dogs roam the streets and overgrown areas of San Antonio each year, but animal experts estimate that only one out of every five can be considered truly homeless. Many of the roaming dogs, feral and semi-domesticated, travel along a series of creek beds, greenbelts, and drainage culverts known as the "dog highway," giving them access to water and the ability to traverse largely unseen between neighborhoods.

In fiscal year 2015 the city's animal shelter received 102,855 service calls for dogs; 10,680 were for locations within five hundred feet of a waterway. "There are a lot of green spaces surrounding the waterways, by virtue of the fact that people are drawn to the scenery and nature," ACS chief field operations officer Shannon Sims said. "So are the animals. It's a natural inclination for them to want to be near water."

It happens all over the city. Alazán Creek runs out of Woodlawn Lake in District Seven, down through a large swath of the West Side in District Five, and south of San Fernando Cemetery No. 1. It meets up with Apache Creek and San Pedro Creek before flowing to the San Antonio River, by the mission's area and the new World Heritage Site on the Southeast Side. Leon Creek flows through District Six into District Four. Salado Creek runs through the East Side in District Two.

ACS officers find dogs roaming in all those areas, with heavier concentrations in the areas of Leon Springs and Balcones Heights and on the East Side, on South New Braunfels Avenue. Most of the dogs seen roaming loose on the streets are essentially community dogs because they're provided food and water by someone or have some other kind of friendly human contact, said Katie Jarl, Texas senior state director for the Humane Society of the United States.

Studies show that those dogs return to the area they consider home every night. "There are very few that are not relying on a human or going to a human," Jarl said. She said roaming dogs often feed off trash or bowls of food set out by well-meaning animal lovers. At South Side Lions Park, for example, people leave buckets filled with water and bowls of scraps of food for the roaming dogs. "So many times, we'll see that the truth is that dog has been walking that street for quite a long time," Jarl said.

While some animal lovers may romanticize roaming dogs as free spirits who are happier living outdoors, animal experts note the semi-domesticated roaming dogs tend to die younger and often fall victim to abuse and illness. They're also more likely to get rabies or other diseases from wild animals they encounter in overgrown areas. "I think the ultimate goal is to have pets inside, being cared for, and people and animals of San Antonio having a great lifestyle," Jarl said.

ACS director Heber Lefgren said the shelter has seen a decrease in resident-initiated calls and that officers have been more proactive in identifying new ways to address the many loose dogs across the city who aren't truly strays. "That's where the focus has been the last couple of years and will continue to be," he said. "We still need to try to educate, inform, and promote the change in behavior that pets' owners need to have in these areas."

According to a city ordinance, anyone who cares for an animal for more than thirty days, including leaving food out for roaming dogs, is legally responsible for that animal. In fiscal year 2015, 29,727 animals were brought into ACS. Of those, 21,046 were dogs, with 13,529 brought in by ACS field officers. In fiscal year 2016 ACS brought in 31,811 animals. Of that number, 23,598 were dogs, and 15,005 were brought in by field officers.

ACS spokeswoman Lisa Norwood said that, overwhelmingly, people bitten by dogs are bitten by animals that belong to somebody; they're not feral. Wild dogs don't come near people, she said. In the course of an investigation into a dog bite, neighbors often confirm where a dog lives or an area it frequents. Residents' input is essential to controlling the roaming dog population, Norwood said.

When ACS officer Robert Lopez drove toward the Salado Creek Greenway one recent evening, a motorist stopped him, saying he'd seen ten dogs along the edge of the park. Minutes later Lopez saw two adult dogs and a pup resting in tall grass. As soon as he approached, the trio slipped into the brush. Holding a forearm in front of his face, he plowed through patches of thick brush, only to find empty dens burrowed into the earth beneath slabs of crumbled concrete in the overgrown area. As Lopez returned to his truck, Kim Ramirez, sixty-three, flagged him down. Holding the leashes of her two terriers, Yucca and Brooks Dale, she told him about another loose dog sighting.

Two years ago Ramirez found the terriers wandering along the greenway and adopted them as her pets. She said people regularly dump animals in the area. She said there have been times when loose dogs have attacked pets in the neighborhood. "I wish there was a big sign that said, 'Spay/neuter your animals.' If you can't love them, don't have them."

About a week earlier, before dusk, ACS officer Sabrina Oyervides stopped by Monterrey Park, where a black Labrador stopped for his daily meals. At the start of summer, workers at the park would leave chicken and hamburgers for him and a brown-and-white Lab mix. ACS field operations supervisor Aimee DeContreras has since brought in the brown-and-white dog, but the black one evaded capture all summer and remains at large as fall settles in. DeContreras has gone back to the area several times.

A crafty canine, the black Lab readily accepts food from visitors but won't go near an officer. The last time she saw him, DeContreras spotted the dog in a grassy area, but before she could get to the curb he had put a good distance between himself and the truck. Before she could park, the dog was already at the corridor's edge. And by the time she opened her door, he had made his way to the creek bed, ambling down the dog highway.

OF COMBAT, CAMARADERIE, AND COUNTRY

A War Bride's Life

Knitting scarves is a hobby that's given ninety-five-year-old Joan Christine Barrera joy through the ups and downs of a life filled with war, disappointment, and, most importantly, love. Each day she sits in her coffee-colored armchair, knitting for hours in the Northeast Side home she shares with her daughter, Catherine Castillo.

She is surrounded by mementos of days gone by from her birthplace of Wotton-under-Edge, England. Cups, steins, and plates commemorating the royal family's history decorate three shelves on a living room wall. A bust of the late prime minister Winston Churchill, topped with a Santa hat, rests on a half-ledge across from her. "I wouldn't be here today if it wasn't for him," Barrera said. "He's the one who saved England—him and President Roosevelt."

On a corner wall hangs a portrait of her late husband, Manuel Barrera, in his army uniform. It's a comforting reminder of the man she fell in love with during the war between the Allies and the Axis forces.

Barrera watches the news of the world on television as she knits. It's been her pastime since she learned the craft at the age of four in school. She still has an English accent, laced with a South Texas drawl. She's woven hundreds of scarves, every color of the rainbow, as gifts for family, friends in England, ladies at church, and the poor. She's knitted shawls and scarves through a clash of cultures, discrimination, and missing the green country pastures of her youth. She taught preschool and played piano at different churches in the area. But knitting has been woven through her life.

"I have had a wonderful life over here with my husband," she said, glancing at his portrait. "I have no complaints."

World War II figured prominently in Barrera's life. She recalled sitting around the radio with her family when Churchill announced that Britain was at war with Germany. She was fifteen when she stood on a knoll at night and saw German planes drop bombs on Bristol, twenty-two miles away.

In April 1944 Barrera and her friend Hazel rode their bicycles to check out the American soldiers posted at the 94th General Hospital at Tortworth Castle. Manuel Barrera, a good-looking soldier, caught the seventeen-year-old's eye. The teens asked him if he knew the way to their town. They knew he'd say no—they just wanted a closer look at the nineteen-year-old from Texas.

A week later she saw him at a local village dance. Barrera was with a soldier from Wisconsin, but that didn't deter her future husband from asking her to dance. She spent the rest of the evening with the man who would become her suitor. They dated for fifteen months, riding bikes through the countryside and stopping at a special bench on Wotton Hill. Manuel Barrera, who worked in the camp kitchen, brought his girlfriend Baby Ruth candy bars and her mother canned chicken.

Manuel proposed to her at their special bench. He asked her mother for her hand in marriage and permission to take her to America. A priest married the couple at Saint Dominic's Catholic Church in Dursley, where they had a three-day honeymoon.

In July 1946 Barrera became one of an estimated seventy thousand war brides to join their husbands in the United States. She and other war wives boarded the *Zebulon B. Vance* army ship for a fifteen-day voyage across the Atlantic to America. The three women she shared a room with all were seasick. Barrera wasn't. She had brown paper pinned under her vest, an old sailor's trick a former seafaring neighbor had recommended that her mother pass on to her.

Barrera traveled from New York for three days by train to San Antonio. Her husband and his sister, Mary, were waiting at the Missouri Pacific Depot for the bride, who wore a camel-hair coat, and a dress made of parachute silk. It was 104 degrees that day.

The couple lived with his aunt Matilda in the Alazán-Apache Courts on the West Side. The next year they moved in with his grandmother, who taught Barrera to speak Spanish and cook traditional recipes.

On her first Christmas with her new husband's family they served tamales, and she cried. She missed the traditional British dinner with mincemeat pies and turkey with dressing. On their way home he stopped and bought her a sandwich.

Barrera recalled that she was taken aback by the discrimination she and her husband faced in the 1950s. They were turned away at the Majestic Theatre and denied an apartment because of her husband's heritage. But airmail letters from her mother every week helped Barrera keep a sense of home. She found support from her husband, his family, and the British Brides Association, a group of British war brides who met once a month. It was through the group that she was able to return to England with her six-year-old son, David.

Castillo called her mother a spitfire whose strong faith keeps her growing. She grew up with Hispanic and British traditions that included festive foods, wearing paper hats, and popping English crackers on New Year's Eve. And there was her mother's traditional British trifle pudding, a layered dessert. "I had the bests of both worlds," Castillo, sixty-four, said. "It's great to grow up in two different worlds."

When fall arrives and temperatures dip, Barrera brings out her yarn and starts knitting. It has been a comfort for what's been a tough year for her. She's overcome health issues, to the delight of her family. Her dearest friends are no longer with her, and COVID-19 has isolated her from one remaining comrade.

But the yarn and the knitting needles are still with her, always within reach to knit more scarves that bring comfort and joy.

World War II Crew Stumbles upon Tuskegee Airmen

The bomber was losing altitude at two hundred feet a minute. Anti-aircraft flak had fused the bomb bays open on a run over an industrial rail center in Linz, Austria. Two of four engines had been hit. Crew 396 faced a dilemma—ditch the plane in the Adriatic Sea or find a place to land within minutes. Nose gunner Michael Preputnik spotted an airstrip on the eastern Italian coast. It wasn't on their maps. The crew thought it had to be a German base. Still, they agreed that being prisoners was better than crashing into the ocean.

The last two engines cut out as pilot 1st Lt. Murl D. Brown landed the damaged bomber. Parked nearby were P-51 Mustangs with painted red tails, like the fighters that protected them on missions. To the crew's surprise, two Black pilots rose from the Mustangs. African American men in U.S. Army uniforms packed four jeeps that rolled up to the bomber. The all-white crew was stunned—the only African American servicemen they had seen during the war were cooks and waiters. They'd landed at Ramitelli Airfield, Italy, the home base of the Tuskegee Airmen—their escorts on bombing runs. The pilots, their faces obscured by helmets, never broke formation, always close through enemy skies.

Twenty-two years ago World War II veteran Larry Fleischer revealed how his crew discovered one of the Army Air Corps' best-kept secrets. Fleischer was a bombardier on the Yellow Oboe, a B-24

Liberator stationed in Southern Italy. Over coffee at a Northeast Side eatery, he rewound time to January 20, 1945, a fateful day he never forgot.

"People don't realize the Tuskegee Airmen saved hundreds of lives," Fleischer said in 2001. "Plus the fact that every time a plane got back and was able to go again was what won the war. We realize what those men did for us. And we want to continue thanking them."

The Tuskegee Airmen served when the military was segregated. The first all-Black military pilot squadron escorted Allied bombers on long-range missions over the Mediterranean and Europe. Named for their training site in Alabama, the airmen are credited with helping integrate the military. When I was starting out as a journalist, Fleischer took an interest in my career, always supportive. We met for several years, sharing tales of our backgrounds. Fleischer was eighteen when he was drafted into the army. He was Jewish, a native of New York City, which teemed with all races.

Fleischer's crew flew twenty-five missions; eight of the twenty-eight bombers on the 1945 Linz mission never made it back to their base in Southern Italy. Bombing runs over Afghanistan stirred memories of military service and prompted him to contact the *San Antonio Express-News* to gauge interest in the story that impacted the crew's lives.

At twenty-five thousand feet, the frigid temperature, 60 degrees below zero, froze his eyes open. Three one-hundred-pound live bombs remained stacked in the bay. Breathing from a portable oxygen bottle, Fleischer crawled into the cramped bay five times to dislodge the ordinance. He lost a boot when his foot got stuck in the racks. Wearing another crewman's boot, he kicked the bombs loose above the Swiss Alps.

Fleischer suffered severe frostbite that was treated at Ramitelli. During their several-day stay, the crew enjoyed the airmen's hospitality—all except for the pilot. He wouldn't sleep on a Black man's cot and spent the first night in the plane, cold from sea air that swept through the bomber. The next night he accepted his hosts' invitation to sleep in one of their warmed tents.

Sgt. George Watson, one of the men in the jeeps, wasn't thrilled about two white enlisted men sleeping in his tent. On a phone call from his home in Lakewood, New Jersey, Watson said that at first his attitude was, "These guys didn't want us in the States. Let them sleep outside."

It wasn't long before he joined bunkmates and the white crew members as they swapped war stories. "That's the first time we were integrated—for a week," he said.

He stayed in contact with ball turret gunner Frank X. Connolly, who said the story was a "living part of our history." Fleischer also kept in touch with fellow crew members. In October 1997 Fleischer, Connolly, and tail gunner Victor DeWolf traveled to Moton Field at Tuskegee and presented a memorial plaque to two original Tuskegee Airmen for saving the bomber crew's lives during the war.

Fifty-two years after his mission, Fleischer was awarded the Purple Heart. He said his hospital records never reached the Pentagon, and the award was denied because his actions took place over the Alps, a neutral location. Eventually efforts by crew members and state senator Gregory Luna resulted in recognition of Fleischer's bravery at a ceremony at Kelly Air Force Base.

It felt fitting that the Purple Heart was pinned on by Gen. Daniel James III, adjutant general of the Texas National Guard and son of original Tuskegee Airman general Daniel "Chappie" James.

After the war Fleischer moved to San Antonio, away from the cold of New York, which caused recurring pain from the frostbite. He worked as a civil engineer at military bases and later practiced law.

Fleischer died on February 13, 2018. He was ninety-three. But our first meeting remains a lasting memory. The World War II veteran opened a manila folder and pulled out an old black-and-white photo of the ten-member crew. The young men, ages eighteen to twenty-four, stand in front of their B-24 Liberator. They're forever young, ready to fly missions high in enemy skies, protected by the war's best-kept secret.

Vietnam Veterans Reunite to Honor Fallen Comrade

The last time these soldiers of Bravo Company, 2nd Platoon, were together, they were tromping through the jungles of Vietnam on enemy patrol. They were the core group of thirty-seven men whom 2nd Lt. Perry Dotson led for four harrowing months in 1970. Forty-nine years later they gathered at a San Antonio hotel to remember a fallen brother-in-arms and renew a connection that time and distance could not break. They came from across the country, bringing wives and children with them.

Present were San Antonio resident Ignacio Amaro, sixty-seven, and his wife, Irene; Edwin "Doc" Ayers, seventy-one, of South Carolina and his daughter, Stacy Ayers Williams; Ernie Levesque, seventy, of Massachusetts; Bill Steele, sixty-eight, of California; Armando Moralez, sixty-eight, of Indiana and his son, Jesus; Tim "Porky" Roland, seventy, of McAllen and his wife, Carmen.

As they walked into the room, the men swarmed Dotson, seventy-one, whom they hold in high regard. He helped them survive those hellish days in 1970, they said, thousands of miles from loved ones. "The camaraderie was something," Levesque said. "You got everybody pulling together."

There was one notable absence among the friends: Pfc. Leonard Nitzsche, killed in action by an enemy sniper in 1970. The reunion gave the Vietnam veterans a safe space to talk and celebrate their survival.

The meeting was set in motion years ago when Dotson sought out Nitzsche's grave site in Chester, Illinois. He said it was his duty to give the private who was in his command the proper farewell he didn't receive when he was felled by a sniper's bullet. He found his first clue online, identifying a cemetery in southern Illinois as Nitzsche's possible resting site.

In October 2017 he traveled to the small town and, with the help of the town clerk and a librarian in Ellis Grove, found the site where Nitzsche was buried. Dotson laid flowers at the tombstone, with a note: "To friends and family of Leonard Nitzsche: 'Len, we all appreciated your courage and selflessness. We will never forget you. Perry Dotson, Leonard's platoon leader.'"

"I don't want to ever lose the pain," he said. "I don't want to lose his memory."

The clerk and librarian also helped him find Nitzsche's relatives. Last year he returned to Illinois to speak with Nitzsche's sister, Linda Rader, and other family members. The completion of his search set off phone calls and texts from other platoon members and relatives.

Roland's wife saw a newspaper story online about Dotson's visit and contacted Rader, who gave her Dotson's phone number. Amaro and Roland had been keeping up with each other over the years. In September, the pair sent a selfie and text to Dotson that read, "Hey Lieutenant... remember us?"

As word spread about a possible reunion, four more joined in. The group of seven convened in San Antonio, where the winters are warm. "It's just a gift to get together," Dotson said. "It's indescribable. You take care of your buddy, we all go home, and that's what these guys did."

The men operated forty miles northwest of Saigon, walking in single file, charged with adrenaline, ready to react to any movement.

They depended on each other and followed the lead of the young lieutenant from Saint Paul, Minnesota.

In October 1969 Dotson had caught a puck hit off hockey star Bobby Orr's stick at a game between the Boston Bruins and the Minnesota North Stars. On patrol, he carried the black disk for luck in the pocket over his heart. Ayers recalled that on his second day in the country, he took off his fatigue shirt and hung it on a tree branch. Dotson told him if he raised up to get it, he would get a round in his head or his chest. The lieutenant slid onto the ground and quickly pulled the shirt down.

"It was a training opportunity," Dotson said. "Fuel them with a little confidence and people survive."

The unofficial mission was fighting to stay alive for 365 days, the length of their tour of duty. "The ultimate goal was to get on the freedom bird and get back to the world," Levesque said.

The men said Nitzsche, a big, quiet farm boy with a slight smile, wanted to be the point man, the soldier who walked up front and kept an eye out for danger. "The guys who walk point, in their hearts they know they're taking care of their buddies," Dotson said. "He wanted to do his share."

On April 8, 1970, the soldiers knew they were near a bunker complex. They were cautious as they walked down a shallow incline, when shots rang out from across a stream. Lynn Becker, the slack man behind Nitzsche, yelled, "Leonard's hit!" Dotson and Roland, the radio man, ran to the front but were pinned down by sniper fire.

"We're not going to leave him here," Dotson recalled the soldiers saying.

With suppressive gunfire from a Cobra helicopter overhead and smoke grenades between them and the bunker, they were able to retrieve the soldier. The men kept an eye out for the enemy as Doc Ayers cleaned the body. Twenty minutes later the helicopter departed with Nitzsche. There was no time to say goodbye to their comrade. The men pushed their grief aside and continued their patrol.

"It was serious business," Ayers said. "A man just died. It brought us closer together."

After the war the men went on with their lives. Ignacio worked for the U.S. Postal Service, Doc became a college professor and counselor, Dotson was a construction executive, Steele became a respiratory therapist, Moralez worked for a phone company, and Levesque drove commercial trucks. They carried the nightmares of the war home with them. They woke up slowly, were wary in areas that looked similar to Vietnam, and grappled with the loss of those who never made it home.

Roland's wife said all she could do was listen and ask how she could take away his pain. Moralez's son said many people have negative thoughts of Vietnam. For him, it's how his mother met his father, who was attending the wedding of a soldier he knew in Vietnam. "I'm actually here because of the war," Jesus Moralez said.

Ayers's daughter said the reunion helped the men settle old anxieties from the conflict. "I think it was really good therapy for all of them," Williams, thirty-five, said. "It was long overdue."

The men still have one more task: to share their meeting with Nitzsche's sister and family. Their goal is to visit his grave site as a group.

"It's amazing to me, the human spirit," Moralez said, his voice breaking. "You do what you have to do."

Straight Out of Omaha

Driving toward the Valley Hi gate at Joint Base San Antonio–Lackland is like entering a tunnel to the past. A building on the right once housed a packed dance floor disco named Daddy Warbucks, where I met my wife forty-five years ago. Up the road was the Donut Hut, home of the best lemon jelly doughnuts. On the right is the 3703rd Basic Military Training Squadron. In 1975 it was a thousand-man dorm at Lackland AFB, where two military training instructors broke down and rebuilt me and forty-seven young men into airmen. It's where, for six weeks of basic training, the sound of metal heel taps striking concrete struck fear in our souls. That sound first scrambled our senses on the last midnight of September.

Hours earlier we'd arrived from inner cities, suburbs, and country towns to San Antonio International Airport. We were part of an all-volunteer military force of two million young men and women months after the Vietnam War ended. I was straight out of Omaha with my high school buddy Brian Simmons.

A sergeant lined us up and led us to a blue shuttle bus that transported us to the Lackland processing center called the Green Monster. He hustled us to a chow hall for eggs, bacon, and the military's go-to, chipped beef on toast, or SOS, an acronym for words unsuitable for print. After breakfast a bus took us to the 3703rd. We lugged suitcases behind our guide, who lined us up at an outside concrete pad beneath the dorm.

We were a sign of the mid-1970s. Afros framed faces, long hair brushed shoulders, and crew cuts rose above clean-cut sides. We wore bell-bottoms, jeans, and church pants. We checked every race and ethnicity on the census, volunteers for a purpose greater than ourselves. We all had one thing in common—no idea what was about to happen. Nervous chatter mixed with calls of insects in the darkness.

Then we heard it—the strike of metal on pavement, like a single raindrop hitting a metal can over and over. Click. Click. Click. The din echoed around the pad, its direction unknown. The source of the mysterious sound rounded the left corner. He was an African American training instructor (TI), a Smokey Bear hat slanted over eyes sunk in shadows. Big as a muscle-bound wrestler, he was a technical sergeant, rumored to be a marine, now in the air force.

He was rage and fury in a tapered shirt, razor-sharp creased pants, and polished black low quarters that dust dared not descend. To this day I have no idea what he yelled for us to do. We picked bags up and put them back down again and again. We jumbled into one another, trying to line up by height as he shouted our names at an ear-splitting level. By the time he ran us up to our dorm, he'd accomplished us doing one thing together—breaking out in a cold sweat. No one slept that night.

The next morning we stared like zombies as bemused barbers shaved our heads as if they were shearing sheep. At the Green Monster airmen sized us up and issued us shoes, blue dress uniforms, and olive-drab fatigues, ill-fitting or not. The TI's Anglo counterpart had a cool demeanor—good cop to rage and fury's bad cop, the perfect combo for shaping us into airmen. He had a thick mustache, like a shorter version of TV's Ted Lasso. With an even tone he told us we'd be okay if we followed their commands. He showed us the art of "midnight requisitions"—a way to secure cleaning supplies from our sister flight.

Rage and fury taught us to count in Japanese, Spanish, and German when we marched. During inspections, no mistake missed his eagle eyes. The center aisle between the two rows of beds was reserved for his and Ted Lasso's tap-heeled shoes. Drills, running, and classes filled our days. We fired an M16 rifle, ran an obstacle course, and yelled "Sir, yes, sir!" We learned about Abraham Maslow's hierarchy of needs, illustrated by a pyramid shape of how needs motivate behavior, lessons that helped immensely during my twenty-two-year career.

We bonded in bays we mopped clear as glass. Promises to stay in touch didn't survive time and distance from when our TIs transformed us from civilians to airmen. For me, those six weeks of reinvention were much needed. Three months before graduating from high school, I had no prospects for my future. A childhood friend strongly suggested I do as he had two years earlier—enlist in the air force. I still salute him for his sage advice.

We graduated intact. Darkness gave way to gray dawn as we boarded a bus to the airport for flights to technical training schools across the country. We were moving on, far from days of drill, regimentation, and the fear-induced sound of taps echoing in the night. As the bus rolled through the back gate, Jefferson Starship's "Miracles" played softly from the driver's transistor radio. To many of us, being on the other side seemed like a miracle.

Military Dependents Experience Different Tales

Living in San Antonio in the late 1960s was a tale of two cities for me and my old friend Larry Mitchell. He lived in Rainbow Hills, appropriately named for the integrated neighborhood. During a phone conversation, he revealed the sting of discrimination I'd never experienced in my area of town. We were both preteens when Martin Luther King Jr. was assassinated.

On the night of April 4, 1968, our mothers, Valeria Cardona-Trinidad and Ruth Mitchell, shed tears for the slain civil rights leader. Larry's tears came after stinging remarks from classmates the next day. "Your king is dead," they yelled. "Now you'll have to go back to Africa!"

Scared and confused, his mother consoled him. It wasn't the last racial incident Larry experienced that year.

He was a standout left-handed first baseman and the only Black player on the Bullets baseball team. At the end of the season he was selected as a Valley Hi Little League all-star. His mother sat at a picnic table under a pavilion at Comanche Park, waiting to see him receive his well-deserved recognition. They called the players' names in alphabetical order. When he heard "Miller," he was ready to walk to the trophy table. But something wrong happened—they'd skipped his name. Larry was distraught.

After the ceremony his mother asked the team coordinator about the slight. The woman said it was a mistake. The next week Larry's mother had him call the official. She said the award wasn't ready yet at the trophy shop. He never received his trophy. "There will be times in your life when people will not respect you, will not give you the dignity you deserve. But you have to keep doing your best in whatever you do," his mother said.

The year 1968 was a time of change—the beginning of the end of our innocence. Our mothers took on double parental duties when our fathers and thousands of military members served in Vietnam. The world morphed from black and white to bright technicolor. Everything was "mod." Radio stations played sweet soul music on the same dial as searing, guitar-driven rock and roll. It was a time when pride in culture, race, and women's rights upended the status quo.

From March 1967 to March 1969 my father was stationed at Kelly Air Force Base. My three sisters and I joined hundreds of military-dependent children who temporarily called San Antonio home. The edge of the western and southwest quadrants was our world, a bubble where life was starkly different from other zip codes in the city.

We lived off Five Palms, on Reefridge Place, where you could hear the echo of barking military training dogs from nearby Lackland Air Force Base. Bands of kids walked to and from school on streets with names like Mossledge Drive and Kontiki Place. Dry, flat scrubland, where we camped around cactus and scraggly mesquite trees, is now the suburbs, lined with watered green lawns.

In 1969 we said our goodbyes to Larry and his family. Our father had been reassigned to Offutt Air Force Base in Omaha, Nebraska. Time again to pack, move, and make new friends. As we drove to Nebraska's largest city, I didn't have a clue that San Antonio would play a pivotal part in my future.

Six years later I returned for basic training at Lackland. In 1978 I returned for five years to the "Gateway to the Air Force" after a two-year assignment at Ramstein Air Base, Germany. When it came time for our family to decide on a place to retire, we chose the Alamo City. It always felt like more than a temporary stop, like home.

Larry's family stayed in San Antonio, where he married, raised a family, and has a successful career as a director of talent acquisition. On a 2020 Zoom call during the COVID-19 pandemic, his team at Airrosti discussed the murder of George Floyd and race relations. Afterward he reached out to team members to check on their well-being as the nation grappled with the pandemic and social unrest.

Larry talked about the four times as an adult that police had pulled him over without cause. He also shared the story about how he never received a trophy as his teammates did fifty-two years earlier.

At a meeting a week later he was shocked. Airrosti executives, chairman Kelly Green and chief population health officer Chris Cato, had a surprise for him. It was a trophy. The inscription read "Valley Hi Little League All-Star—Larry Mitchell." Gratitude for the duo's kindness prompted the tears he shed that day, not bigotry or bias.

"It was delayed," Larry said of the long-awaited honor, "but not denied."

Acknowledgments

Many thanks to the folks, mentors, and groups who offered their unwavering support over the years.

Thanks to Dee Dixon for the phone call that made a career in journalism possible; Kym Fox for opening the door of opportunity and giving me a chance to find my way; Craig Thomason for hiring and setting me on the path to becoming a reporter; Anne Marie Kilday, Arthur Moczygemba, and Barry Robinson for their side-by-side approach that laid the foundation to reporting. Thanks to the San Antonio Association of Black Journalists and Society of Professional Journalists and the San Antonio Association of Hispanic Journalists for their encouragement and support.

Thanks to Carolina Garcia and the Freedom Forum Diversity Institute, especially Wanda Lloyd and Robbie Morganfield for their tutelage. Thanks, also, to Robert Rivard and Brett Thacker for their support to strengthen my reporting skills while I was studying at Texas State University.

Lorna Stafford encouraged me to pursue working in the newsroom and dig a little bit deeper to find the real story. Diana Fuentes offered years of counsel and experience as a consummate reporter who always stressed making one more call and employing attention to detail so a story sang.

Jeanne Russell and Nicole Foy's guidance and friendship paved the way to writing without fear.

Elaine Ayala assigned my first freelance feature stories and many other assignments that helped hone my reporting skills. Terry Bertling supported my story ideas over the years. Anita Baca taught me how to see stories through a cinematic lens. Veronica Flores-Paniagua's support saw me through rough patches.

Carmina Danini shared a host of stories and showed me how to juggle and research several at a time. Arthur Santana taught me the art of interviewing, to let a scene unfold without interruption, and to seek those living on the margins of society.

Thanks to Monica Markel for giving us license to comb the city for stories tucked away, out of sight of the daily blur of hustle and bustle, and to June Wormsley for believing I could reach a higher level of reporting.

Guillermo Garcia, Lety Laurel, and Lisa Harrison offered calm counsel when my confidence flagged.

Pod mates Vianna Davila, Michelle Mondo, and Lomi Kriel demonstrated the highest degree of journalism in their reporting and offered many hours of sage advice. And I appreciate the constant encouragement by Fauzeya Rahman and Brittney Martin for reality checks.

Many thanks to Roger Downing, Robert Kolarik, and John Hamilton for their style lessons and edits of my Saturday stories.

I'm forever indebted to publisher Mark Medici and editor-in-chief Marc Duvoisin, executive editor Nora Lopez, and metro editor Greg Jefferson, who gave me the opportunity to have a weekly column sharing narratives of San Antonio's everyday people.

Many thanks to my colleagues at the *San Antonio Express-News* over the years who contributed immensely to my career.

I'm eternally grateful to the many photojournalists who contributed greatly to helping me develop interviewing skills in the early years of reporting.

And thank you to the copy editors and editors, especially Barry Harrell, Henry Krausse, and Julie Silva, who encouraged me to share my journey in columns, just as the folks did who opened their hearts about lives of joy and pain.

A big thank-you goes out to Tom Payton, Burgin Streetman, Sarah Nawrocki, and the staff at Trinity University Press; it was great to work with you all. And much gratitude to Emily Jerman Schuster for shaping and refining the manuscript with her expertise and eye for detail.

A big shout-out to my Omaha brothers, Lonzale Ramsey, Willie Richardson, Frederick Montgomery, Andrew Baran, Robert Reams, and Kenneth Pollard, for support during our ongoing journey.

Last but not least, I'm grateful to the readers who took time to read these tales. Thank you. I couldn't have had this second career without you.

A twenty-two-year air force veteran, **Vincent T. Davis** started at the *San Antonio Express-News* in 1999 as a part-time city desk editorial assistant, working nights and weekends while he attended San Antonio College and worked on the staff of the campus newspaper, the *Ranger*. He completed a three-month Freedom Forum Diversity Institute fellowship at Vanderbilt University in 2003 and earned his bachelor's degree in communication design from Texas State University in 2006.

www.ingramcontent.com/pod-product-compliance
Lightning Source LLC
Jackson TN
JSHW021108180126
96542JS00001B/1

* 9 7 8 1 5 9 5 3 4 3 3 4 5 *